STORYTIME THEME-A-SAURUS®

The Great Big Book of Storytime Teaching Themes

By **Jean Warren**

Illustrated by **Barb Tourtillotte**

Pattern Illustrations by **Judy Shimono**

Totline
PUBLICATIONS

Warren Publishing House
A Division of Frank Schaffer Publications
Torrance, California

Some of the activity ideas in this book were originally submitted by *Totline Newsletter* subscribers. We wish to acknowledge the following contributors: Connie Clayton, Monahans, TX; Barbara Downing, Wilmington, NC; Ruth Engle, Kirkland, WA; Judy Hall, Wytheville, VA; Barb Johnson, Decorah, IA; Debra Lindahl, Libertyville, IL; Kathy McCullough, Everett, WA; Judith McNitt, Adrian, MI; Joleen Meier, Marietta, GA; Rose C. Merenda, Warwick, RI; Susan A. Miller, Kutztown, PA; Ann M. O'Connell, Coaldale, PA; Susan M. Paprocki, Northbrook, IL; Kay Roozen, Des Moines, IA; Diane Thom, Maple Valley, WA.

Editorial Manager: Kathleen Cubley
Editor: Elizabeth McKinnon
Copy Editor: Brenda Mann Harrison
Contributing Editor: Gayle Bittinger
Editorial Assistant: Erica West
Production Manager: JoAnna Brock
Art Director: Jill Lustig
Book Design/Layout: Sarah Ness
Cover Design: Eric Stovall
Cover Illustration: Elizabeth Read/Carol DeBolt

Theme-A-Saurus® is a registered trademark of Warren Publishing House.

ISBN 0-911019-56-1

Library of Congress Catalog Card Number 92-64377
Printed in the United States of America
Published by: Warren Publishing House

Business Office: 23740 Hawthorne Blvd.
Torrance, CA 90505

Introduction

Storytime Theme-A-Saurus contains my adaptations of 12 classic folktales and fables.

I must admit that the stories I chose for this collection happen to be among my favorites. I also looked for stories that were simple, easy for young children to dramatize and lent themselves to theme units.

To make the stories more appropriate for very young children, I tried to create a balance of male and female character roles. I also shortened some of the stories and deleted frightening parts when necessary.

Following each story are easy, hands-on activity suggestions for art, language, learning games, movement, music, science or social studies, and snacks. Each story is also followed by a set of patterns designed to be reproduced and used for making flannelboard cutouts and other learning aids.

When working with a story unit, feel free to pick and choose activities. Perhaps all you may have time for is to read the story and sing a song or serve a related snack.

Take your lead from your children. If they seem to want to expand their story experience into other learning areas, such as art, movement or science, you can let them do the activities in the book or provide them with activities you have developed yourself.

It is my pleasure to share these stories with you. I hope that it won't be long before they become favorites with your children.

Jean Warren

Contents

The Big, Big Carrot

An adaptation of "The Big, Big Turnip"
By Jean Warren

Once upon a time a girl planted a tiny carrot seed.

Soon, the seed sprouted. Every day the girl watered it and watched as the green leaves grew bigger and bigger.

Her baby sister wanted to help, but the girl said she was much too small to grow carrots.

One day, the girl went out to her garden to pull up the carrot. But try as she might, it was stuck too tight.

She called to her father, who was mowing the grass.

"Father dear, come here, come here,
I've pulled with all my might.
I can't pull my carrot out,
It's stuck so very tight!"

So the father came running. He grabbed on to the girl and they both pulled and pulled, but the carrot was stuck too tight.

The father turned and called to the mother, who was hanging out the clothes.

"Mother dear, come here, come here,
We've pulled with all our might.
We can't pull this carrot out,
It's stuck so very tight!"

So the mother came running. She grabbed on to the father and they all pulled and pulled, but the carrot wouldn't budge.

Next, the mother turned and called to the brother, who was riding around on his bike.

"Brother dear, come here, come here,
We've pulled with all our might.
We can't pull this carrot out,
It's stuck so very tight!"

So the brother came running. He grabbed on to the mother and they all pulled and pulled, but the carrot wouldn't move an inch.

Next, the brother turned and called to the grandfather, who was washing the car.

"Grandfather dear, come here,
come here,
We've pulled with all our might.
We can't pull this carrot out,
It's stuck so very tight!"

So the grandfather came running. He grabbed on to the brother and they all pulled and pulled, but the carrot was still stuck tight.

Then the grandfather turned and called to the baby sister, who was playing with her wagon.

"Baby dear, come here, come here,
We've pulled with all our might.
We can't pull this carrot out,
It's stuck so very tight!"

So the baby sister came running. She grabbed on to the grandfather and they all pulled and pulled — and out popped the carrot!

Everyone clapped for the baby sister because she was the greatest help of all.

The carrot was big and long, and the girl was happy to let her baby sister help carry it to the house in her wagon.

Printing With Carrots

Select carrots of various sizes. Cut several of them crosswise into thick rounds and cut others lengthwise into halves or fourths. Place folded paper towels in shallow containers and pour on small amounts of orange tempera paint. Let your children dip the carrot pieces into the paint and press them on pieces of construction paper to create carrot prints.

Family Portraits

Give each child a piece of white construction paper. Set out crayons or felt-tip markers. Talk about the different family members who helped the girl in "The Big, Big Carrot." Then ask your children to draw pictures of people in their own families who would help them if they were the girl in the story.

Extension: Cut frames for your children's Family Portraits from posterboard or cardboard. Let the children decorate their frames as desired. Then attach the children's pictures to the back sides of their frames.

Three Little Carrots

Recite the poem below and let your children name the rhyming word at the end of each verse.

Three little carrots,
What can I make?
I'll use one
To make a carrot cake.

Two little carrots,
Just watch my carrot tricks.
I'll chop one
To make some carrot sticks.

One little carrot,
Alone in the sink.
I'll blend one
To make a carrot drink.

Jean Warren

Extension: Ask your children to tell what dishes they would make if they had some carrots. Write down their "recipes" and put them together to make a group "carrot cookbook."

Family Opposites Game

Ask your children to answer the following questions about the members of their families: "Who is the largest? The smallest? Who is the tallest? The shortest? Who is the youngest? The oldest?"

Flannelboard Fun

Make copies of the patterns on pages 15-18. Color the patterns and cover them with clear self-stick paper, if desired. Then cut them out and glue felt strips on the backs. Encourage your children to use the pattern cutouts on a flannelboard to retell the story "The Big, Big Carrot."

Carrot Game

Select 6 to 10 carrots of various sizes. Cut off the leafy tops. Let your children take turns lining up the carrots from largest to smallest or from shortest to longest. When the game is over, wash the carrots and save them for use in the carrot recipes on page 14.

Pulling Up Carrots

Purchase about 10 carrots with green, leafy tops. Plant the carrots in a big tub of dirt so that they look as if they are actually growing. Ask one child to pull up two carrots, another child to pull up four carrots, a third child to pull up one carrot, and so on, until the tub is empty. Then replant the carrots and start the game again.

Role-Playing Fun

Let your children act out the story "The Big, Big Carrot." Add other family members (a grandmother, an uncle, a cousin, etc.) as needed so that everyone can have a part. Have the girl who first tries to pull up the carrot hold on to a stationary object while the other family members hook on behind her.

Wagon Hauling

Obtain a small wagon. Let your children take turns using it to haul items around inside or outdoors. Whenever you need something moved from one place to another, give it to a child to haul in the wagon. Or have the children use the wagon to give rides to stuffed animals or one another.

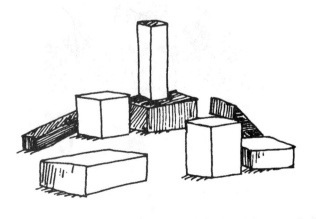

Down in My Garden
Sung to: "Down by the Station"

Down in my garden
Early in the morning,
See my big carrot
Stuck so tight.
See all the people
Come to help me pull,
Tug, tug, tug, tug,
With all our might!

Jean Warren

Grow, Grow, Little Carrots
Sung to: "Row, Row, Row Your Boat"

Grow, grow, little carrots,
Growing in a row.
I will take good care of you,
I'll water you just so.

Have the children walk back and forth as they sing, pretending to water carrots.

Jean Warren

Growing Carrots

Explain to your children that carrots are root vegetables and that we eat the part of the plant that grows underground. Then help the children prepare a space for a carrot garden in a sunny spot outdoors. Show them how to plant carrot seeds in rows. Have them water the garden regularly, and help them to thin the rows when the sprouts begin to appear. Encourage the children to weed their garden as necessary. When the carrots are ready to be pulled up, let the children decide how they would like to prepare them for eating.

Carrot Sequence Cards

Make copies of the carrot sequence cards on page 19 and color them. Cover the cards with clear self-stick paper for durability, if desired, and cut them out. Mix up the cards and let your children take turns arranging them in the proper order.

Extension: If desired, make a fifth card that shows cooked carrots on a plate.

Carrot Bread

1 cup whole-wheat flour
1 teaspoon baking powder
½ teaspoon baking soda
2 teaspoons cinnamon
¼ teaspoon salt
½ cup raisins
3 tablespoons unsweetened apple-
  juice concentrate
1 egg
¼ cup vegetable oil
1 teaspoon vanilla
1 ripe banana, sliced
1 cup finely grated carrot

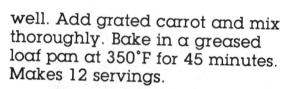

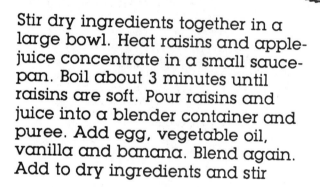

Stir dry ingredients together in a large bowl. Heat raisins and apple-juice concentrate in a small saucepan. Boil about 3 minutes until raisins are soft. Pour raisins and juice into a blender container and puree. Add egg, vegetable oil, vanilla and banana. Blend again. Add to dry ingredients and stir well. Add grated carrot and mix thoroughly. Bake in a greased loaf pan at 350°F for 45 minutes. Makes 12 servings.

Variation: To make muffins, pour batter into a greased 12-cup muffin tin and bake at 350°F for 35 minutes.

Carrot Sticks and Dip

Let your children help wash fresh carrots. Peel the carrots and cut them into sticks. Serve them with a favorite dip or use the dip recipe that follows.

Cottage Cheese Dip — In a blender container, place 1 pint cottage cheese, ⅓ cup milk and ½ package onion or vegetable soup mix. Blend until smooth and creamy. Refrigerate for at least 30 minutes before serving.

The Big, Big Carrot 15

The Big, Big Carrot

The Big, Big Carrot   19

The City Mouse and the Country Mouse

Adapted by Jean Warren

Once upon a time there were two mouse cousins. One lived in the city and the other lived in the country.

One day, the city mouse went to visit her cousin in the country.

When she arrived at her cousin's house, she was surprised to see how small and plain it was.

The country mouse was happy to see her city-mouse cousin. She took her past the fat sleeping cat and into her small room in the wall behind the kitchen table.

The country mouse set out a dinner of cheese and bread and asked her cousin to join her.

"Is this all you have to eat?" asked the city mouse. "How can you put up with such poor food? Come with me to the city. I will show you how to really live."

So the two cousins set off down the road.

As they got closer and closer to the city, the traffic got heavier and heavier.

The country mouse held on tighter and tighter to her cousin's hand when they had to cross a street.

At last, they reached the city mouse's home. It was a beautiful, big house.

The city mouse led the way through a hole in the kitchen door and took the country mouse into a large dining room.

The table was covered with the remains of a feast.

Soon, the mice were filling up on pies, cakes, jellies and other goodies. The country mouse thought it was all very grand.

Suddenly, they heard loud growling and barking. Two huge dogs ran into the room.

The city mouse cried, "Follow me!" Quickly she ran across the table, down the table leg and into a hole in the wall.

The country mouse followed as fast as she could, escaping the dogs by only a second.

The next day, the country mouse thanked her cousin for the visit but said that she was going home. As she left, the country mouse explained, "I would rather eat cheese and bread in peace than pies and cakes in fear."

FINE APPAREL

BAKERY

Mouse Tails

Cut several mouse body shapes for each child out of gray construction paper. Let your children glue pieces of yarn to their mouse shapes for tails. Then have them glue their mice on pieces of light-colored construction paper. Let them add eyes and other details with crayons or felt-tip markers.

Collage of Homes

Cut pictures of city houses, country houses, etc., from magazines and home-buyers catalogs. Give your children a large piece of paper and some glue. Let them choose house pictures and glue them on the paper any way they wish to create a Collage of Homes. Encourage the children to tell which houses they would most like to live in and why.

Mouse Story

Make up a story about a city mouse and a country mouse who were complete opposites. Include sentences such as those that follow and let your children fill in the blanks: "If the city mouse ran up the stairs, the country mouse ran _____ the stairs. If the city mouse went in the door, the country mouse went _____ the door. If the city mouse went over the fence, the country mouse went _____ the fence. If the city mouse walked fast, the country mouse walked _____."

Flannelboard Fun

Make copies of the patterns on pages 29-30. Color the patterns and cover them with clear self-stick paper, if desired. Then cut them out and glue felt strips on the backs. Encourage your children to use the pattern cutouts on a flannelboard to retell the story "The City Mouse and the Country Mouse."

Travel Game

Place three or four familiar objects in a small suitcase. Have your children sit with you in a circle. Let one child open the suitcase, look at the objects inside and then close it. Then have the child say, "I'm going on a trip to the (country/city) today and I'm taking (names of the three or four objects)." Continue in the same manner until everyone has had a turn. Make the game easier or more challenging by putting a smaller or larger number of objects into the suitcase.

Who Lives Where?

Make copies of the game cards on page 31 and color them. Cover the cards with clear self-stick paper for durability, if desired, and cut them out. Mix up the cards and let your children take turns pairing the animal pictures with the pictures of the animal homes.

Thumbprint Mice Number Books

Give each child five large index cards that have been numbered from 1 to 5. Let your children use commercial ink pads to make a matching number of black thumbprints on each card. When the ink has dried, have the children turn their thumbprints into mice by using black felt-tip markers to add eyes, ears, whiskers and tails. Then staple each child's cards together to create a book. If desired, add covers to the books for the children to decorate.

Sneaky Mice

Ask your children to pretend that they are little mice. Have them show you how they would scamper about and wiggle their noses and whiskers. (Remind them to be very, very quiet in case a cat or a dog happens to be nearby.) Then let the children take turns leading expeditions around the room to find pretend food.

Role-Playing Fun

Let your children act out the story "The City Mouse and the Country Mouse." Choose several children to pretend to be the cat and the dogs. Divide the rest of the children into two groups and let them be city mice and country mice.

Extension: If desired, make mouse noses by cutting small circles out of black construction paper and gluing on whiskers cut from gray construction paper. Attach the circles to the children's noses with loops of tape rolled sticky side out.

Country Mouse and City Mouse Song
Sung to: "Frere Jacques"

Country mouse, country mouse,
Simple food, simple house.
Running round the cat
Asleep upon the mat.
Country mouse — what a house!

City mouse, city mouse,
Fancy food, fancy house.
Running night and day
From the dogs at play.
City mouse — what a house!

Jean Warren

Three Country Mice, Three City Mice
Sung to: "Three Blind Mice"

Three country mice, three country mice,
See how they run, see how they run.
They run around the farm all day,
They munch on cheese and hide in the hay,
They're careful the cat doesn't see them play.
Three country mice.

Three city mice, three city mice,
See how they run, see how they run.
They run around most of the night,
Hiding from dogs that are quite a sight,
They nibble on cakes but they feel such fright.
Three city mice.

Jean Warren

City Life, Country Life

Look through magazines to find pictures of city items and scenes and pictures of country items and scenes. Cut out the pictures and place them in a pile. Let your children sort the pictures into two groups: one that represents city life and one that represents country life.

Extension: Let your children glue the pictures on two long pieces of butcher paper titled "City Life" and "Country Life." Display the papers on a wall or a bulletin board.

Floor Map

Show your children a few simple maps. Talk with them about how we can use maps to help us locate places. Then draw a pretend road map of a city and a country area on a piece of butcher paper. Include pictures of landmarks such as skyscrapers, stores, houses, farms and trees. Tape the map to the floor and set out toy cars. Let your children have fun driving the cars from the city to the country and back again.

Country Mouse Snacks

Select several kinds of cheese. Cut the cheese into small squares (or cubes) and arrange them on a platter. Set out small squares of two or three different kinds of bread. Give your children paper plates. Let them help themselves to the cheese and bread squares that they would like to sample.

City Mouse Snacks

Let your children help make little jelly-filled pies, using the recipe that follows.

1 cup all-purpose flour
½ teaspoon salt
4 tablespoons margarine, softened
2 tablespoons water
Jelly

In a mixing bowl, stir together the flour, salt, margarine and water. Form dough into little balls and make a deep thumbprint in each one. Bake on a baking sheet at 350°F for 20 to 25 minutes. When cool, fill thumbprint holes with jelly. Makes 16 to 18 pies.

The City Mouse and the Country Mouse 29

30   The City Mouse and the Country Mouse

The City Mouse and the Country Mouse 31

The Elves and the Shoemaker

Adapted by Jean Warren

Once there lived a very poor shoemaker and his wife. All they had was just enough leather to make one last pair of shoes.

The shoemaker cut out the leather for the shoes, then he and his wife went to bed.

In the morning, much to their surprise, they found the shoes already made and stitched to perfection.

The shoemaker's wife placed the shoes in their shop window and quickly sold them at top price.

With the money they received, the shoemaker bought enough leather to make two pairs of shoes.

He cut out the leather for the shoes in the evening, then he and his wife went to bed.

Again, when they awoke in the morning, they found the shoes already made and finely stitched.

The shoemaker's wife placed the two pairs of shoes in the shop window, and again they were quickly bought by happy customers.

This time the shoemaker had enough money to buy leather for four pairs of shoes.

Once more he cut out the leather before bedtime, and again the shoes were finished in the morning.

Soon, the shoemaker and his wife were no longer poor.

One evening just before Christmas, the shoemaker and his wife decided to stay up all night to find out who was doing the good work. They set out a candle for light and hid behind a curtain.

At midnight, two little elves danced into the shop. They were poorly dressed, especially for winter time, but they quickly set to work, hammering and tapping, sewing and snapping. By morning, all the shoes were finished, and the elves danced out the door.

The next day, the shoemaker and his wife decided to do something nice for the elves. The shoemaker set to work making them fine leather shoes. The shoemaker's wife spent all day making them splendid green pants and red vests.

That night, the shoemaker and his wife placed the tiny new shoes and clothes on the workbench and went to bed.

When the elves came, they were delighted with the gifts! They put on the new clothes, danced around the room once, and then danced out the door.

The elves never returned. But the shoemaker and his wife were never poor again, and they were always thankful for the help that the two elves had given them.

Printing With Shoes

Collect old athletic shoes or tennis shoes in small sizes. Set out a piece of butcher paper and pour various colors of tempera paint into large shallow pans. Let your children dip the soles of the shoes into the paint and press them all over the butcher paper to create prints. When the paint has dried, display the paper on a wall or a bulletin board.

Glitter Shoes

Find several old pairs of men's and women's shoes. Have your children cover the shoes with glue, place them in shallow box lids and then sprinkle them with glitter. When the glue has dried, tap the excess glitter off the shoes to save for another project. Let the children wear their Glitter Shoes for dress-up play or on special occasions.

Making Slippers

Help each of your children make a pair of slippers to wear. Have the child take off his or her shoes and stand on a piece of cardboard. Trace around the child's feet and cut out the shapes to use for slipper soles. Cut out and trim two wide strips of vinyl to fit over the top parts of the child's feet, as shown in the illustration. With the strips in place, punch holes along the edges of the slippers as shown. Then let the child lace yarn or string through the holes to fasten the parts of the slippers together.

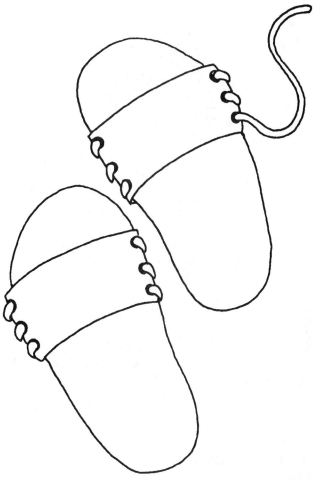

Elf Finger Puppets

Photocopy the elf finger puppet on page 43 for each child. Glue or tape the puppets to index cards for sturdiness and cut them out. Also cut out the finger holes as indicated by the dotted lines. Show the children how to make legs for their puppets by sticking their fingers through the finger holes. Have them move their fingers up and down to make their elf puppets dance.

Five Pairs of Shoes

Use the pattern on page 43 as a guide to cut one pair of shoe shapes from each of these colors of felt: red, blue, yellow, green and black. Place the pairs of shoes on a flannelboard. As you read the following poem, let your children take turns removing the appropriate pairs.

Five pairs of shoes
By the cobbler's door.
Someone bought the red ones,
Now there are four.

Four pairs of shoes
For all to see.
Someone bought the blue ones,
Now there are three.

Three pairs of shoes
Shiny and new.
Someone bought the yellow ones,
Now there are two.

Two pairs of shoes
Sitting in the sun.
Someone bought the green ones,
Now there is one.

One pair of shoes
Oh, what fun!
Someone bought the black ones,
Now there are none.

Jean Warren

Flannelboard Fun

Make copies of the patterns on pages 41-42. Color the patterns and cover them with clear self-stick paper, if desired. Then cut them out and glue felt strips on the backs. Encourage your children to use the pattern cutouts on a flannelboard to retell the story "The Elves and the Shoemaker."

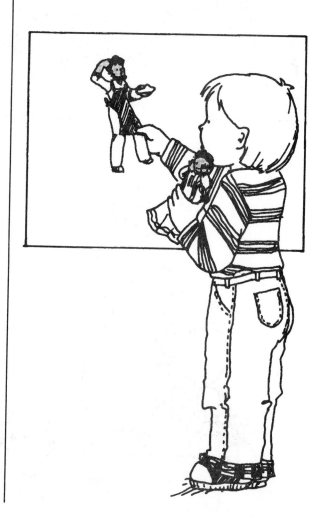

Sorting Shoes

Place 10 to 20 pairs of shoes in a large box. Include a wide variety of kinds and sizes. Set out the box and let your children sort the shoes in different ways. For example, have them sort the shoes into pairs. Then let them sort the shoes by color, size, texture, type of fastener, etc.

Counting by Twos

Sit with your children and line up five pairs of shoes. Count the shoes, one by one, up to 10. Then show the children how to count the 10 shoes by twos. Have them count with you as you point to one pair of shoes at a time. Ask: "Which way of counting is faster, by ones or by twos?"

Role-Playing Fun

Let your children act out the story "The Elves and the Shoemaker." Choose two children to be the shoemaker and his wife and let all the others be elves. If desired, set out dress-up clothes for the children to wear and play music for the elves to dance to.

Tap, Tap, Tap

Have your children sit on the floor in a circle. Ask them to imagine that they are cobblers and their arms are hammers. Start by saying "Tap, tap, tap" very slowly, pausing between words. Have the children pound their fists on the floor each time you say "tap." Gradually speak faster until everyone is tapping at a rapid rate. Then let each child have a turn leading the tapping movements.

How Would You Walk?

Have your children pretend that they are putting on different kinds of shoes. Ask them to show how they would walk or dance in cowboy boots, galoshes, ballet slippers, athletic shoes, tap shoes, high heels, thong sandals, etc.

Down at the Shoe Store
Sung to: "Down by the Station"

Down at the shoe store,
Early in the morning,
See the little shoes
Standing in a row.
See the happy customers
Coming in to buy them.
Ooo! Ahh! Ooo! Ahh!
Off they go.

Jean Warren

Someone's Making Brand-New Shoes
Sung to: "She'll Be Coming Round the Mountain"

Someone's making brand-new shoes, yes, they are.
Someone's making brand-new shoes, yes, they are.
They are tapping all night long,
Making shoes new and strong.
Someone's making brand-new shoes, yes, they are.

We will hide tonight and see them, yes, we will.
We will hide tonight and see them, yes, we will.
They are tapping all night long,
Making shoes new and strong.
We will hide tonight and see them, yes, we will.

It's the elves who are working, yes, it is.
It's the elves who are working, yes, it is.
They are tapping all night long,
Making shoes new and strong.
It's the elves who are working, yes, it is.

Jean Warren

The Elves and the Shoemaker 39

Shoe Store

Set up a play Shoe Store in a corner of your room. Supply it with several chairs, pairs of shoes in shoe boxes and a ruler or a metal foot-measuring tool from a local shoe store. Let your children take turns being sales clerks and customers.

Red and Green Snacks

After reading "The Elves and the Shoemaker," talk with your children about the new red and green clothes that the shoemaker's wife made for the elves. Then provide the children with red and green snacks such as tomato and lettuce salads, red and green bell-pepper slices, red and green apple slices or small bowls of red and green gelatin.

The Elves and the Shoemaker 41

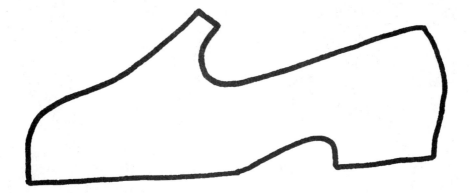

The Elves and the Shoemaker 43

The Gingerbread Kid

An adaptation of "The Gingerbread Boy"
By Jean Warren

Once upon a time there lived a farmer and his wife who had no children.

One day, the farmer's wife was feeling very lonely, so she decided to bake a gingerbread kid.

She mixed some gingerbread dough and then rolled it out gently. Next, she carefully cut out a large gingerbread kid.

She placed it on a cookie sheet, put it into the oven, and waited patiently for it to brown.

When she saw that the gingerbread kid was done, she opened the oven and took it out.

It was perfect. Now she would no longer be lonely.

Then much to her surprise, the gingerbread kid jumped off the cookie sheet and began running around the room.

The farmer's wife was thrilled. It was just like having a real child.

But when she went to pick up the gingerbread kid, it said, "Run, run — you can't catch me! I'm a gingerbread kid. I'm free, I'm free!"

Then the gingerbread kid ran out the door.

The farmer's wife chased after the gingerbread kid, but it was too fast for her. It ran on and on to the field where the farmer was working.

When the farmer tried to catch the gingerbread kid, it said, "Run, run — you can't catch me! I'm a gingerbread kid. I'm free, I'm free!"

The farmer and his wife both chased after the gingerbread kid, but it was too fast for them.

It ran on and on past a cow, a pig and a hen. They all tried to catch the gingerbread kid, but it was just too fast.

At last, the gingerbread kid came to a pond where it had to stop. "Oh me, oh my," it said. "What shall I do now? I can't get wet."

Just then, out of the bushes stepped a sly fox. "Climb onto my back," he said. "I will give you a ride across the pond."

The gingerbread kid jumped onto the back of the fox.

When they reached the middle of the pond, the fox lowered his back into the water. "Quick," he cried, "climb up onto my big nose! The water is deeper here."

As the gingerbread kid quickly climbed up onto the fox's nose, the fox said, "Yum, yum, look what I caught for me! One gingerbread kid, and it's free, it's free!"

Then in one gulp, he gobbled up the gingerbread kid. And that is the end of this story.

Gingerbread Kid Costumes

Make gingerbread kid costumes for your children. For each one, cut an extra-large gingerbread kid shape out of brown construction paper. Cut a large face hole in the center of the head. Open a large grocery bag, turn it upside down, and cut a matching face hole out of one of the wide sides. Then glue the gingerbread kid shape to the side of the bag so that the face holes are matched up. Let your children decorate their costumes as desired before they slip them over their heads and shoulders.

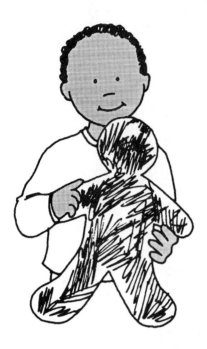

Finger-Painted Gingerbread Kids

Let your children finger-paint on pieces of butcher paper with brown paint. Allow the papers to dry. Then cut the papers into large gingerbread kid shapes.

Extension: Set out decorating materials such as buttons, rick-rack, yarn segments and fabric scraps. Give your children the gingerbread kid shapes and let them glue on the decorating materials any way they wish. Attach the finished gingerbread kids to a wall or a bulletin board.

Five Gingerbread Kids

Cut five gingerbread kid shapes out of brown felt and place them on a flannelboard. As you read the following poem, let your children take turns removing the felt shapes.

Five gingerbread kids
Cooling by the door.
A cow ate one,
Then there were four.

Four gingerbread kids
Running by the tree.
A pig ate one,
Then there were three.

Three gingerbread kids
By a pond so blue.
A fox ate one,
Then there were two.

Two gingerbread kids
Running in the sun.
A hen ate one,
Then there was one.

One gingerbread kid
Running for its life.
It ran away
From the farmer's wife.

Jean Warren

Flannelboard Fun

Make copies of the patterns on pages 53-54. Color the patterns and cover them with clear self-stick paper, if desired. Then cut them out and glue felt strips on the backs. Encourage your children to use the pattern cutouts on a flannelboard to retell the story "The Gingerbread Kid."

Math Counters

Make a small cardboard gingerbread kid pattern. Trace around
the pattern on brown posterboard to make 20 or more gingerbread kid shapes. Cut out the
shapes and give them to your
children to use for various counting games.

Color Sorting

Cut 12 gingerbread kid shapes
out of brown posterboard or cardboard. Divide the shapes into
three equal sets. Using colored
plastic tape, make and attach
red bow ties to the first set, yellow bow ties to the second set
and blue bow ties to the third set.
Place the shapes in a box and
spread out red, yellow and blue
construction paper. Let your children sort the gingerbread kids by
placing them on the papers that
match the colors of their bow ties.

Story Sequence Cards

Make copies of the story sequence cards on page 55 and color them. Cover the cards with clear self-stick paper for durability, if desired, and cut them out. When your children are familiar with "The Gingerbread Kid," give them the sequence cards. Let them take turns arranging the cards in the proper order.

Gingerbread Kid Puzzle

Using felt-tip markers, draw a large gingerbread kid shape on a piece of brown posterboard or cardboard. Add a face and other details as desired. Cut the shape into 4 to 12 interlocking puzzle pieces, depending on the ages and abilities of your children. Identify the back side of each puzzle piece with a check mark. Then mix up the pieces and let your children take turns putting the puzzle together.

Gingerbread Cookies, Run Around

Let your children pretend that they are gingerbread kid cookies. Recite the following poem several times and have the children act out the movements described.

Gingerbread cookies,
Run around.
Gingerbread cookies,
Touch the ground.
Gingerbread cookies,
Around you go.
Gingerbread cookies,
Now — go — slow.

Jean Warren

Role-Playing Fun

After reading the story "The Gingerbread Kid," act out parts of the story with your children. For example, assume the role of the farmer's wife and let the children pretend to be small balls of gingerbread cookie dough. Have them lie flat as you roll over them with an imaginary rolling pin and then cut them into gingerbread boys and girls. After you pretend to bake them in an oven, have them try moving one leg, then the other; one arm, then the other. Then have them stand up, take a few small steps, and finally start to run as you chase after them.

Run, Run, You Can't Catch Me
Sung to: "Twinkle, Twinkle, Little Star"

Run, run, you can't catch me,
I run too fast, as you can see.
I outran the farmer, I outran his wife,
I'll outrun you 'cause I run for my life.
Run, run, you can't catch me,
I run too fast; I'm free, I'm free!

Jean Warren

Gingerbread
Sung to: "Three Blind Mice"

Gingerbread, gingerbread,
Um, um, good! Um, um, good!
I like to make it day or night.
I like to gobble it up in one bite.
If it ran away, that would be a sight!
Gingerbread.

Jean Warren

Gingerbread Kids

1½ cups all-purpose flour
½ cup whole-wheat flour
½ cup wheat germ
2 teaspoons baking soda
2 teaspoons ground ginger
2 teaspoons ground cinnamon
¼ teaspoon ground cloves
2 egg whites, lightly beaten
1 cup unsweetened apple-juice
  concentrate, divided
¼ cup vegetable oil

Stir together dry ingredients in a large mixing bowl. Stir in egg whites and half of the apple-juice concentrate. Heat remaining apple juice until hot. Add hot juice and the oil to batter. Mix well. Spread out dough, about ¾-inch thick, on a greased baking sheet. Bake 30 to 35 minutes at 350°F. Let cool. Then cut out Gingerbread Kids using a child-shaped cookie cutter.

What Dissolves in Water?

Talk with your children about why the gingerbread kid in the story was afraid of crossing the pond. (It would have dissolved if it had gotten wet.) Then set out a tub of water along with water-soluble and non-soluble items such as salt, pudding mix, a cookie, a slice of bread, a carrot, a spoon, a piece of paper, a wood block and a rubber band. Let your children choose items, predict whether or not they will dissolve, and then place them in the tub of water to see what happens.

The Gingerbread Kid 53

The Gingerbread Kid 55

The Hare and the Tortoise

Adapted by Jean Warren

Once upon a time there was a hare who liked to boast about how fast he could run.

One day, a tortoise heard the hare boasting and she offered to race him.

"Sure," agreed the hare, as he laughed to himself. I can easily outrun her, he thought.

So the hare and the tortoise decided where the race would start and where it would end. Then they asked an owl to be the referee.

When the hare and the tortoise were at the starting line, the owl said, "Ready — set — go!"

And off the two animals went.

Soon, the hare was far ahead of the tortoise. In fact, he was so far ahead that he decided to stop for a short nap.

"That tortoise is so slow," he said. "Even if she catches up to me, I can easily run past her again."

56

The hare lay down and was soon fast asleep.

The tortoise crawled on and on. Eventually she came to where the hare was sleeping.

"Oh my, he looks peaceful," she said. "It wouldn't be nice to wake him." And she crawled on toward the finish line.

When the hare woke up, he looked all around. But he couldn't see the tortoise anywhere.

"That slow tortoise still hasn't caught up to me," he said.

But when the hare neared the end of the race, he got a surprise. There sat the tortoise, already on the finish line.

She was the winner!

After that day, the hare was not so boastful about how fast he could run. He had learned that being slow and steady can also win a race.

Rabbit Ears

Let your children help make Rabbit Ears to wear. Give them each a paper plate. Have them use crayons or felt-tip markers to color the center parts of the plates pink.

Then cut each plate as indicated by the dotted lines in the illustration. Fold up the pink "ears" as shown before slipping the rims of the plates over the children's heads.

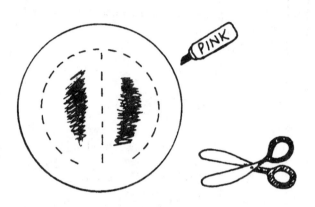

Turtle Shells

Make a "turtle shell" for each of your children by cutting a head hole out of the bottom of a large brown paper bag and arm holes out of the sides of the bag. Let the children paint their shells green or brown. When the paint has dried, help the children put on their Turtle Shells. Encourage them to crawl on the floor like turtles.

Flannelboard Fun

Make copies of the patterns on pages 65. Color the patterns and cover them with clear self-stick paper, if desired. Then cut them out and glue felt strips on the backs. Encourage your children to use the pattern cutouts on a flannelboard to retell the story "The Hare and the Tortoise."

Puppet Fun

Give each of your children a rabbit shape and a turtle shape cut from construction paper. (See patterns on page 66.) Let the children decorate their shapes with crayons or felt-tip markers. Attach craft-stick handles to the shapes to create puppets. Draw a "racecourse" on a piece of butcher paper attached to a wall or a bulletin board. Let the children act out the story "The Hare and the Tortoise" by moving their puppets along the racecourse.

Open-Ended Stories

Ask each of your children to complete these sentences: "When I go fast, I feel like _____. When I go slow, I feel like _____." Write each child's sentences on separate pieces of paper and let the child illustrate them. Then fasten the children's papers together to make two group books, one titled "Going Fast" and the other "Going Slow." Place the books in your book corner for the children to "read" in their free time.

Story Sequence Cards

Make copies of the story sequence cards on page 67 and color them. Cover the cards with clear self-stick paper for durability, if desired, and cut them out. When your children are familiar with "The Hare and the Tortoise," give them the sequence cards. Let them take turns arranging the cards in the proper order.

Hare and Tortoise Board Game

Make a game board by drawing a winding "racecourse" on a large piece of posterboard or cardboard. Mark off a starting line and a finish line and divide the racecourse into segments. Add pictures of grass, flowers and other details to the game board, if desired. Invite two of your children at a time to play the game. Give one a counter to represent the Hare and give the other a counter to represent the Tortoise. Have the children place their counters at the starting line. Let one child begin by rolling a die, naming the number that comes up and then moving his or her counter that many spaces along the racecourse. Then let the other child have a turn. Have the children continue playing until both the "Hare" and the "Tortoise" have crossed the finish line.

Role-Playing Fun

Let your children take turns acting out the story "The Hare and the Tortoise." Or let half of the group be hares and the other half be tortoises. As you read or tell the story, pause to allow time for the children to dramatize the action. When you have finished, let the children switch roles and act out the story again.

Extension: Have your children wear their Rabbit Ears and Turtle Shells from the activities on page 58 while they act out the story.

Fast and Slow

Select several pieces of music that have fast and slow tempos. Ask your children to listen carefully as you play the musical pieces. Have them hop like rabbits whenever they hear a fast tune and crawl like turtles whenever they hear a slow tune. Continue as long as interest lasts.

The Hare and the Tortoise
Sung to: "The Farmer in the Dell"

The hare ran so fast,
The hare ran so fast.
Heigh-ho, the derry-oh,
The hare ran so fast.

The tortoise crawled so slow,
The tortoise crawled so slow.
Heigh-ho, the derry-oh,
The tortoise crawled so slow.

The hare stopped to rest,
The hare stopped to rest.
Heigh-ho, the derry-oh,
The hare stopped to rest.

The tortoise won the race,
The tortoise won the race.
Heigh-ho, the derry-oh,
The tortoise won the race.

Jean Warren

Did You Ever?
Sung to: "Did You Ever See a Lassie?"

Did you ever see a hare,
A hare, a hare,
Did you ever see a hare
Who runs so fast?
He zips and zaps,
And zooms right on past.
Did you ever see a hare
Who runs so fast?

Did you ever see a tortoise,
A tortoise, a tortoise,
Did you ever see a tortoise
Who crawls so slow?
She knows she's low,
Her legs will not grow.
Did you ever see a tortoise
Who crawls so slow?

Jean Warren

Likes and Differences

Display large pictures of a rabbit
and a turtle or a tortoise. Have
your children look closely at the
pictures. Then ask them to tell how
the two animals are alike (they
both have four legs, they both
have a tail, etc.) and how they
are different (the rabbit is covered
with fur but the turtle is covered
with a shell, etc.). If desired, write
down the children's statements
and use them to make a group
book about rabbits and turtles.

Which is faster... a bike or car?

Which Is Faster?

Talk with your children about
things that go fast and things
that go slow. Ask questions such
as these: "Which is faster, a bike
or a car? A jet plane or a scooter?
A turtle or a horse?" Then ask:
"Which is slower, a snail or a
kitten? A trike or a truck? A bird
or a worm?" Encourage the children to make up similar questions, if desired.

Pear Bunnies

For each of your children, place a pear half flat side down on a lettuce leaf. In the narrow end of the pear, insert whole cloves for eyes and almond halves for ears. At the other end of the pear, place a spoonful of cottage cheese for a fluffy tail.

Note: Have your children remove the cloves before eating their pear bunnies.

Turtles

Use a favorite recipe to make banana bread (or any kind of quick bread). Bake the bread in tin cans and let it cool. Then slice it into 1/4-inch-thick rounds. Let your children spread the rounds with softened cream cheese. On each round, place a walnut half to represent a turtle shell. Let the children place raisins around the walnut halves to make heads, legs and tails for their turtles.

Variation: Use crackers instead of bread rounds.

The Hare and the Tortoise 65

66   **The Hare and the Tortoise**

The Hare and the Tortoise   67

Henny Penny

Adapted by Jean Warren

One sunny autumn day, Henny Penny was walking down the road when — thump! — something fell on her head.

"Oh, dear me," said Henny Penny, "The sky is falling! I must go and tell the king." And off she ran.

Along the way she met Ducky Lucky.

"Why are you running?" asked Ducky Lucky.

"I'm off to tell the king that the sky is falling!" said Henny Penny.

"Oh, dear me," said Ducky Lucky, grabbing his umbrella and holding it over his head. "May I come with you?"

"Yes," said Henny Penny, "But we must hurry."

So Henny Penny and Ducky Lucky ran to tell the king that the sky was falling.

Along the way they met Goosey Loosey.

"Why are you running?" asked Goosey Loosey.

"We're off to tell the king that the sky is falling!" said Henny Penny and Ducky Lucky.

"Oh, dear me," said Goosey Loosey, grabbing her old hat and putting it on her head. "May I come with you?"

"Yes," they said. "But we must hurry."

So Henny Penny, Ducky Lucky and Goosey Loosey ran to tell the king that the sky was falling.

Along the way they met Turkey Lurkey.

"Why are you running?" asked Turkey Lurkey.

"We're off to tell the king that the sky is falling!" said Henny Penny, Ducky Lucky and Goosey Loosey.

"Oh, dear me," said Turkey Lurkey, grabbing his three-legged stool and placing it on top of his head. "May I come with you?"

"Yes," they said. "But we must hurry."

So Henny Penny, Ducky Lucky, Goosey Loosey and Turkey Lurkey ran to tell the king that the sky was falling.

Just before they reached the king's palace, they stopped to rest.

"Henny Penny," her friends said, "why don't you cover your head, too?"

"Oh, it's not really necessary," said Henny Penny. "The sky just falls in little pieces, like this." And she held out the small piece of sky that had fallen on her head.

"That's not a piece of sky," said Ducky Lucky, Goosey Loosey and Turkey Lurkey. "That's an acorn, you silly hen!"

The animals all had a good laugh when they realized what had happened. Then they walked back home in the warm autumn sunshine.

Autumn Leaf Prints

Give each of your children two pieces of plain white paper, a paintbrush and a leaf. Set out tempera paint in autumn colors. Have the children brush paint all over the back sides of their leaves. Then have them place their leaves, painted sides down, on one of their papers. Have them place the other pieces of paper on top of their leaves and lightly rub across their papers with their hands. Help the children remove the top papers and leaves to reveal their Autumn Leaf Prints.

Finger-Painted Sky Pictures

Give each of your children a piece of butcher paper with some blue finger paint placed in the center. Let the children spread the paint all over their papers with their hands to make blue sky pictures. Encourage them to use their fingers to make designs in the paint. Allow the papers to dry. Then let the children dip their fingertips into brown paint and press them on their sky pictures to create "falling acorns."

Hat Collages

Use the pattern on page 79 as a guide to cut large hat shapes out of construction paper. Have your children look through magazines and catalogs to find small pictures of different kinds of hats. Let them tear or cut out the pictures and glue them on their hat shapes any way they wish. Display the completed hat collages on a wall or a bulletin board.

Wallpaper Hats

Provide each of your children with two 20-inch squares of wallpaper. Have the children brush glue all over the backs of both of their squares. Help them place the glue sides of their squares together and show them how to press out any excess glue. Have the children stand in front of a mirror, one at a time, and place their damp squares on top of their heads. Help them shape their squares into hats. Tie a string band around each hat to help keep its shape. When the hats have dried, remove the strings and cut the brims into the desired shapes. Set out decorating materials, such as ribbons, bows, artificial flowers and small feathers, and let the children glue them on their hats.

The Sky is Falling

As you read the poem that follows, pause just before the end of each verse and let your children name the rhyming color word.

"The sky is falling!" someone said.
It was the hen colored red.

"I never heard such a bellow,"
Said the duck colored yellow.

"I never saw such a sight,"
Said the goose colored white.

"The sky just can't be falling down,"
Said the turkey colored brown.

"It's most bizarre, that's what I think,"
Said the pig colored pink.

"I think I'll run right home and pack,"
Said the dog colored black.

"It's all a mistake, it isn't true!"
Said the sky colored blue.

Jean Warren

Rhyming Names

Point out to your children that the characters in the story "Henny Penny" all have rhyming names. Using your own name, demonstrate how you can add a rhyming word; for example, "Kathy Pathy" or "Christy Misty." Let the children have fun saying their own names and adding rhyming words. If desired, use the children's rhyming names to make a book for your book corner.

Flannelboard Fun

Make copies of the patterns on pages 77-78. Color the patterns and cover them with clear self-stick paper, if desired. Then cut them out and glue felt strips on the backs. Encourage your children to use the pattern cutouts on a flannelboard to retell the story "Henny Penny."

What's Under the Hat?

Invite your children to sit with you in a group. Set out five or six small toys or other objects and ask the children to name each one. Then have the children close their eyes while you hide one of the objects under a hat. When the children open their eyes, let them try guessing which object is under the hat. Let the child who first guesses correctly hide a different object under the hat for the next round of the game. Continue until each child has had a chance to hide an object.

Sorting Nuts

Set out a basket containing a variety of unshelled nuts such as walnuts, almonds, hazelnuts, pecans and Brazil nuts. Add some unshelled peanuts to the basket, if desired. Let your children take turns sorting the nuts by kind. Then let them line up the nuts from smallest to largest or from largest to smallest.

Role-Playing Fun

Let your children take turns acting out the story "Henny Penny" while you narrate. Each time you prepare to reread or retell the story, have the children who are pretending to be Ducky Lucky, Goosey Loosey and Turkey Lurkey find objects in the room to use for protective head coverings. Then substitute the names of the chosen objects for those mentioned in the story.

Henny Penny
Sung to: "This Old Man"

Henny Penny, walking by,
Felt something fall down from the sky.
And that is why she's running
To the king,
And why this song we sing.

Ducky Lucky saw his friend run by,
She warned him about the sky.
And that is why they're running
To the king,
And why this song we sing.

Goosey Loosey saw her friends run by,
They warned her about the sky.
And that is why they're running
To the king,
And why this song we sing.

Turkey Lurkey saw his friends run by,
They warned him about the sky.
And that is why they're running
To the king,
And why this song we sing.

Down the road, there they go,
Covering their heads like so,
And crying out about the sky,
"It is falling! My, oh, my!"

Include verses about other animals such as Piggy Wiggy or Doggy Loggy, if desired.

Jean Warren

Gravity

Select a variety of unbreakable objects ranging in weight from heavy to very light. Position the objects in front of your children. Hold up one object at a time and ask them to predict what will happen when you drop it. Then let go of the object and have the children observe as it falls down. At the end of your experiment, ask the children if they have heard the word *gravity*. Explain that the force of gravity was what caused the objects to fall downward when they were dropped.

Hard and Soft

Set out a variety of hard and soft materials such as a baking sheet, a plastic plate, a cardboard square, a piece of plywood, a paper napkin, a fabric square, a piece of aluminum foil and a piece of waxed paper. Let your children experiment with the materials to determine which ones would give the best protection from a falling acorn or other small object.

Ground Nut Snacks

Let your children help grind peanuts, walnuts or other kinds of nuts in a nut grinder. Mix the nuts with shredded apple or softened margarine. Then let the children spread the ground nut mixture on crackers or small squares of toast.

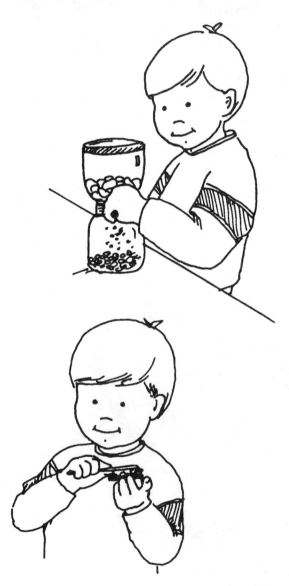

Corn Bread

1 egg
½ cup unsweetened apple-juice
   concentrate
½ cup milk
¼ cup vegetable oil
1 banana, sliced
1 cup all-purpose flour
1 tablespoon baking powder
½ teaspoon salt
1 cup yellow cornmeal

Blend first five ingredients together in a blender container. Stir dry ingredients together in a mixing bowl. Add liquid ingredients and stir. Pour into a greased 8-inch baking pan and bake at 400°F for 25 to 30 minutes. When cool, cut into 2-inch squares. Makes 16 squares.

Henny Penny 77

Henny Penny   79

The Little Red Hen

Adapted by Jean Warren

Once upon a time a little red hen was out in the barnyard with her friends.

She spotted a grain of wheat on the ground, and that gave her an idea.

"Who will help me plant this wheat?" she asked.

"Not I," said the duck.
"Not I," said the mouse.
"Not I," said the pig.

"Then I'll plant it myself," said the little red hen. And she did.

The grain of wheat sprouted and grew into a tall plant. Soon it was yellow and ripe.

"Who will help me cut this wheat?" asked the little red hen.

"Not I," said the duck.
"Not I," said the mouse.
"Not I," said the pig.

"Then I'll cut it myself," said the little red hen. And she did.

When the wheat was cut, the little red hen asked, "Who will help me thresh the wheat?"

"Not I," said the duck.
"Not I," said the mouse.
"Not I," said the pig.

"Then I'll thresh it myself," she said. And she did.

When the wheat was ready to be ground into flour, the little red hen asked, "Who will help me grind the wheat?"

"Not I," said the duck.
"Not I," said the mouse.
"Not I," said the pig.

"Then I'll grind it myself," said the little red hen. And she did.

When the wheat was ground into flour, the little red hen asked, "Who will help me make some bread?"

"Not I," said the duck.
"Not I," said the mouse.
"Not I," said the pig.

"Then I'll make it myself," said the little red hen. And she did.

When the bread was baked, the little red hen asked, "Who will help me eat the bread?"

"I will," said the duck.
"I will," said the mouse.
"I will," said the pig.

"No, you won't," said the little red hen. "I'll eat it myself."

She called to her chicks: "Cluck, cluck. Come here, come here. I made this bread myself, and we're going to eat it all up. Eat up! Eat up!" And they did.

Flour and Water Art

Cut large bread-slice shapes out of heavy brown paper bags or brown construction paper. Give one shape to each of your children. Combine all-purpose flour with water to make a mixture that is the consistency of finger paint and add a little salt for texture. Let the children finger-paint with the flour-and-water mixture on their bread-slice shapes. While the mixture is still wet, have the children sprinkle on wheat berries (see Learning About Wheat on page 87). Place the bread-slice shapes on a flat surface to dry, anchoring the corners with heavy objects to prevent curling.

Barnyard Pictures

For each of your children, draw a simple barnyard scene on a piece of construction paper. Set out colored ink pads and rubber stamps in the shapes of farm animals (a pig, a duck, a cow, etc.). If available, include a stamp of a hen (or a chicken) and a red ink pad. Let the children use the stamps to make prints of farm animals all over their Barnyard Pictures.

Flannelboard Fun

Make copies of the patterns on page 89. Color the patterns and cover them with clear self-stick paper, if desired. Then cut them out and glue felt strips on the backs. Encourage your children to use the pattern cutouts on a flannelboard to retell the story "The Little Red Hen."

Little Red Hen's Bread Book

Ask your children to tell you how they would make bread. Write down each child's "recipe" on a large index card. Then give the cards to the children to illustrate with crayons or felt-tip markers. (Or have them stamp red hen prints across the tops of their recipe cards.) Fasten the cards together with staples or metal rings to make a book. Include a cover and the title "Little Red Hen's Bread Book." Give the book to the children and encourage them to "read" their bread recipes to one another.

Five Loaves of Bread

Cut five bread-loaf shapes out of brown felt and place them on a flannelboard. Then recite the following rhyme and have your children take turns removing the shapes. As you come to the end of each verse, encourage all the children to name the rhyming number word.

Five loaves of bread cooling by the door,
(Child's name) took one, now there are four.

Four loaves of bread, I hope there's one for me,
(Child's name) took one, now there are three.

Three loaves of bread, now just a few,
(Child's name) took one, now there are two.

Two loaves of bread, I guess I'd better run,
(Child's name) took one, now there's only one.

One loaf of bread, will I be the lucky one?
(Child's name) took it, now there are none.

Jean Warren

Sequence Cards

Make copies of the story sequence cards on page 90 and color them. Cover the cards with clear self-stick paper for durability, if desired, and cut them out. When your children are familiar with "The Little Red Hen," give them the sequence cards. Let them take turns arranging the cards in the proper order.

Extension: Copy the patterns on page 91 to make bread-making sequence cards. After discussing how bread is made, let your children arrange the cards in the correct sequence.

Role-Playing Fun

After reading the story "The Little Red Hen," talk with your children about how the hen planted the wheat, cut it, threshed it, ground it, and made it into bread. Then ask the children to pretend that they are all little red hens in the barnyard. Read or tell the story again. Each time you say the line "And she did," have the children act out the appropriate movements. At the end of the story, encourage them to act out eating the bread.

Making Bread
Sung to: "Frere Jacques"

Making bread, making bread,
Ummm, good. Ummm, good.
I can smell it baking,
I can smell it baking.
Smells so good, smells so good!

Making bread, making bread,
Ummm, good. Ummm, good.
Now it's time for tasting,
Now it's time for tasting.
Tastes so good, tastes so good!

Elizabeth McKinnon

Once There Was a Little Red Hen
Sung to: "The Mulberry Bush"

Once there was a little red hen,
Little red hen, little red hen.
Once there was a little red hen,
Who found a grain of wheat.

"Who will help me plant this wheat,
Plant this wheat, plant this wheat?
Who will help me plant this wheat?"
Asked the little red hen.

"We can't help you plant the wheat,
Plant the wheat, plant the wheat.
We can't help you plant the wheat,"
Said the little hen's friends.

"Who will help me cut the wheat,
Cut the wheat, cut the wheat?
Who will help me cut the wheat?"
Asked the little red hen.

"We can't help you cut the wheat,
Cut the wheat, cut the wheat.
We can't help you cut the wheat,"
Said the little hen's friends.

"Who will help me thresh the wheat,
Thresh the wheat, thresh the wheat?
Who will help me thresh the wheat?"
Asked the little red hen.

"We can't help you thresh the wheat,
Thresh the wheat, thresh the wheat.
We can't help you thresh the wheat,"
Said the little hen's friends.

"Who will help me grind the wheat,
Grind the wheat, grind the wheat?
Who will help me grind the wheat?"
Asked the little red hen.

"We can't help you grind the wheat,
Grind the wheat, grind the wheat.
We can't help you grind the wheat,"
Said the little hen's friends.

"Who will help me make the bread,
Make the bread, make the bread?
Who will help me make the bread?"
Asked the little red hen.

"We can't help you make the bread,
Make the bread, make the bread.
We can't help you make the bread,"
Said the little hen's friends.

"Who will help me eat the bread,
Eat the bread, eat the bread?
Who will help me eat the bread?"
Asked the little red hen.

"We will help you eat the bread,
Eat the bread, eat the bread!
We will help you eat the bread!"
Said the little hen's friends.

"Sorry, but it's just for me,
Just for me and my family.
Sorry, but it's just for me!"
Said the little red hen.

Jean Warren

Learning About Wheat

Purchase wheat berries (available at health food stores). Soak a spoonful of the wheat grains in water overnight. The next day, set out the softened grains and some dried grains for your children to examine with a magnifying glass. Cut some of the softened grains in half so the children can see that each kernel has a brown coat (the bran) and a white starchy center.

Discuss how wheat is ground to make flour. Then demonstrate by grinding a handful of the dried wheat berries in an electric coffee grinder or a blender. Explain that the flour you have made is whole-wheat flour. White flour is made from wheat that has the bran and wheat germ (part of the starchy center) removed.

Sprouting Wheat

Give each child a small bowl. Have your children fold paper towels, place them inside their bowls, and pour on small amounts of water. Then let them sprinkle wheat berries (see Learning About Wheat on this page) on top of the wet towels. Enclose the bowls in clear plastic bags and place them in a warm, sunny spot. When the grains sprout and green stems appear, remove the plastic bags and have the children add water to their bowls regularly.

Extension: Let your children experiment with growing wheat berries in soil.

Homemade Bread

Use a favorite recipe to make white or whole-wheat bread and let your children help with the kneading. If you have never made bread before, check a bread cookbook for step-by-step instructions. Be sure to start early enough in the day so that the children can enjoy eating the warm bread with butter when it comes out of the oven.

Variation: Bake bread using frozen bread dough.

Bread Sticks

1 package yeast
1½ cups warm water (105°F to 115°F)
½ teaspoon sugar
4½ cups all-purpose flour
1 egg yolk
2 tablespoons cold water
Sesame seeds, optional

Dissolve yeast in warm water and add sugar. Add flour and knead 6 minutes. Let dough rise, covered, in a greased bowl until double in size. Divide dough into equal pieces and let your children roll the pieces into sticks of similar lengths. Blend egg yolk with cold water and have the children brush the mixture on their Bread Sticks. Let them sprinkle on sesame seeds, if desired. Place Bread Sticks on a baking sheet and bake at 450°F for 12 minutes.

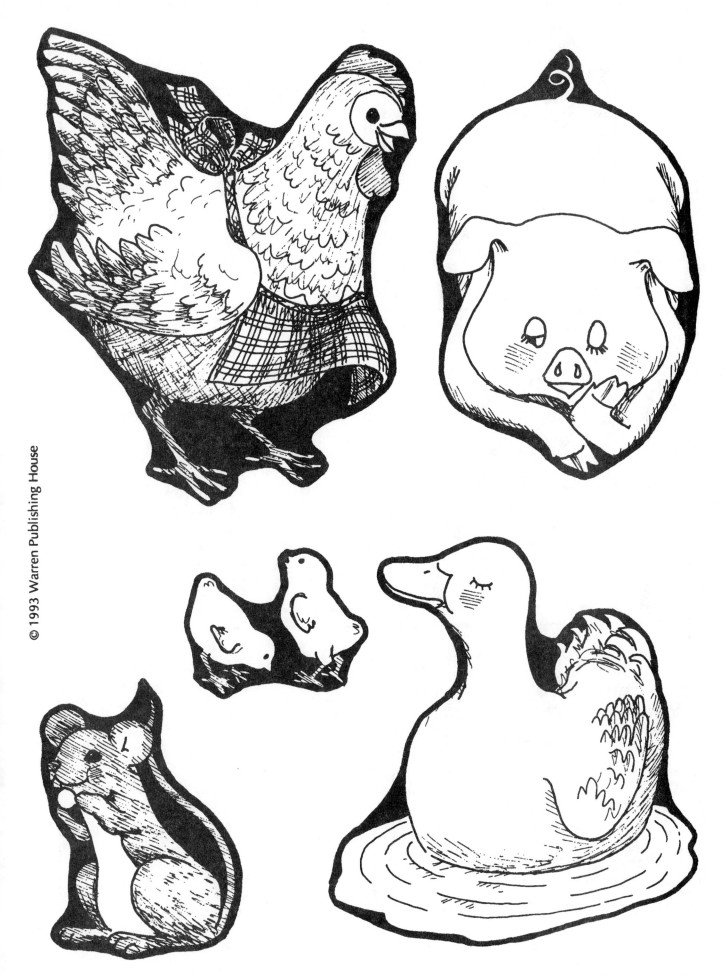

The Little Red Hen   89

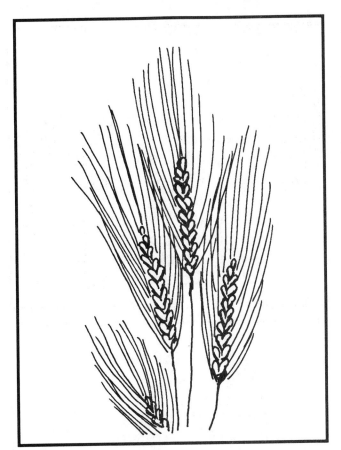

The Little Red Hen   91

Little Red Riding Hood

Adapted by Jean Warren

Once upon a time there was a little girl who always wore a red cape. She was called Little Red Riding Hood.

One day, Little Red Riding Hood baked some cookies for her sick grandmother. She put them into a basket and set off on the path through the woods to her grandmother's house.

When she had gone half-way, Little Red Riding Hood met a wolf.

"Where are you going?" asked the wolf.

"To Grandmother's house," said Little Red Riding Hood. "It's on the other side of the woods."

"Well, I must not keep you," said the wolf. "Have a nice visit." And off he ran to Grandmother's house through a shortcut in the woods.

When Little Red Riding Hood arrived at her grandmother's house, she knocked on the door and said, "Grandma, it's I, Little Red Riding Hood. I've brought you some cookies."

"Come in, my dear," called a deep voice.

Oh my, thought Little Red Riding Hood, Grandma must be very sick to sound so bad.

When Little Red Riding Hood went inside, she saw someone lying in bed. "Grandma," she exclaimed, "what big arms you have!"

"All the better to hug you with, my dear."

"But Grandma," said Red Riding Hood, "what big eyes you have!"

"All the better to see you with, my dear."

"But Grandma," said Red Riding Hood, "what big ears you have!"

"All the better to hear you with, my dear."

"But Grandma," said Red Riding Hood, "what big teeth you have!"

"All the better to eat you with!" cried the wolf, as he jumped up from the bed and grabbed Little Red Riding Hood.

Just then, the door flew open and in came a woodsman carrying his ax. The wolf let go of Little Red Riding Hood and ran out the door as fast as he could.

Little Red Riding Hood was very glad to see the woodsman. Together, they looked around the house and soon found Red Riding Hood's grandmother safe and sound in the closet.

The grandmother made a pot of tea. Then they all sat down and ate the cookies that Little Red Riding Hood had brought.

Little Red Riding Hood had learned a lesson. Never again did she talk to strangers or walk alone through the woods.

Baskets for Grandma

Use the pattern on page 103 as a guide for cutting a large basket shape from construction paper for each child. Set out magazines and small containers of glue. Have your children look through the magazines to find pictures of things that they would like to give to their grandmothers (or other relatives). Let them tear out the pictures and glue them on their basket shapes. When the children have finished, encourage them to talk with one another about the pictures they chose for their baskets.

Red Collages

Set out glue and large pieces of red construction paper. Have your children look through magazines to find red pictures. Then let them tear or cut out the pictures and glue them all over their papers to make Red Collages.

Variation: Let younger children choose from precut pictures that have been placed in a box.

Paper Cookies

Give your children large cookie shapes cut from light-brown construction paper. Let them make "cookie sprinkles" by using a hole punch to punch small circles out of other colors of paper. Have the children brush glue all over their cookie shapes and then add the colorful sprinkles.

Playdough Basket and Cookies

Set out brown playdough. Let your children use part of the dough to make long snakes. Help them coil their snakes together to create a basket. Next, have the children roll small pieces of the playdough into balls and flatten them with their hands to make cookies. Let them put their cookies into the playdough basket.

Grandma Book

Ask your children to complete the sentence "Grandmas are _____." Write each child's response across the bottom of a piece of white construction paper. Let the children decorate the top parts of their papers with crayons. Then fasten the papers together with a colorful cover to make a book. Title the book "Grandmas Are...." (Or let the children choose a title.) Place the book in your book corner for the children to "read" in their free time.

Flannelboard Fun

Make copies of the patterns on pages 101-102. Color the patterns and cover them with clear self-stick paper, if desired. Then cut them out and glue felt strips on the backs. Encourage your children to use the pattern cutouts on a flannelboard to retell the story "Little Red Riding Hood."

Symbolic Story Props

Sit in a circle with your children. Explain that you want to tell the story of Little Red Riding Hood but you don't have any props. Ask: "What could we use for Red Riding Hood?" Accept any object the children suggest as long as it relates in some way (a red vase, a doll with red hair, etc.). Continue by asking the children to suggest items to represent Red Riding Hood's basket, her cookies, the wolf, and so on. When you have a complete set of symbolic props, let the children help place them in order as you tell the story.

Red Color Game

Give each of your children a small paper bag to color with red crayons or felt-tip markers. Ask each child to secretly find a small red object in the room and hide it inside his or her bag. (Make sure there are red blocks, toys, crayons, etc., placed around the room where the children can see them.) Invite the children to sit with you in a circle. Let each child have a turn giving clues about the object inside his or her bag while the others try to guess what it is. Continue until everyone has had a turn.

Basket Game

Set out a variety of baskets. Let your children take turns lining them up from smallest to largest or from largest to smallest. Then have them count how many baskets there are all together.

Variation: Let the children sort the baskets by size, shape, color, type of wicker, etc.

Role-Playing Fun

Provide your children with props to use for acting out the story "Little Red Riding Hood." Include items such as these: a red cape, a red hood and a basket for Red Riding Hood; a headband with paper wolf ears attached for the wolf; a shawl and a nightcap for the grandmother; an outdoor vest or a plaid shirt for the woodsman. Encourage the children to take turns reenacting the story during playtime.

Going to Grandmother's House

Designate a spot on one side of the room to be Little Red Riding Hood's house and a spot on the opposite side to be Grandmother's house. Have all but one of your children stand between the two houses to represent trees. Let the one child start at Red Riding Hood's house and walk through the "woods" any way he or she wishes to get to Grandmother's house. Then have the child become one of the trees and let another child walk through the woods. Continue until everyone has had a turn.

There Goes Red Riding Hood
Sung to: "Row, Row, Row Your Boat"

There goes Red Riding Hood,
Skipping through the woods.
She's happy and merry,
And nothing is scary.
Oh me, oh my, that's good.

Red's granny's not feeling well,
Just looking, one can tell.
Those teeth and that nose
Are the cause of Red's woes.
She ran off with a yell.

So don't walk into the unknown,
First call on the telephone.
And go with your mother,
Your dad or big brother,
But don't go off alone!

Ann M. O'Connell

Little Red Riding Hood
Sung to: "Ten Little Indians"

Little Red Riding Hood,
Little Red Riding Hood,
Little Red Riding Hood
Baked some cookies for Grandma.

Then she skipped down the path,
Then she skipped down the path,
Then she skipped down the path,
Through the woods to Grandma's.

Additional verses:

Halfway there, she met a wolf,
Who asked the way to Grandma's.

When she got to Grandma's house,
She knocked and called to Grandma.

"Come right in, the door's unlocked,"
Called her dear old grandma.

"Grandma, what big eyes you have!"
"The better to see you with."

"Grandma, what big ears you have!"
"The better to hear you with."

"Grandma, what big teeth you have!"
"The better to eat you up!"

Then the wolf jumped off the bed
And grabbed Red Riding Hood.

Just then, a woodsman came
And scared away the wolf.

Everything worked out just fine,
For Red Riding Hood and Grandma.

Jean Warren

Taste Test

Let your children have fun experimenting with their sense of taste. Select three different kinds of popular cookies. Place bite-size pieces of each kind in a separate basket. Cover the three baskets with cloth napkins or towels. Pass around one of the baskets. Have the children reach into the basket with their eyes closed, take out cookie pieces, and try to identify the cookies by taste. Follow the same procedure with the other two baskets.

Variation: For a sugarless alternative, use crackers instead of cookies.

Red Riding Hood Snacks

Serve red snacks after reading "Little Red Riding Hood." Include foods such as tomato soup, red apple slices, cranberry juice, red bell-pepper rings or strawberries. If desired, let your children help set the snack table with red placemats and red paper napkins.

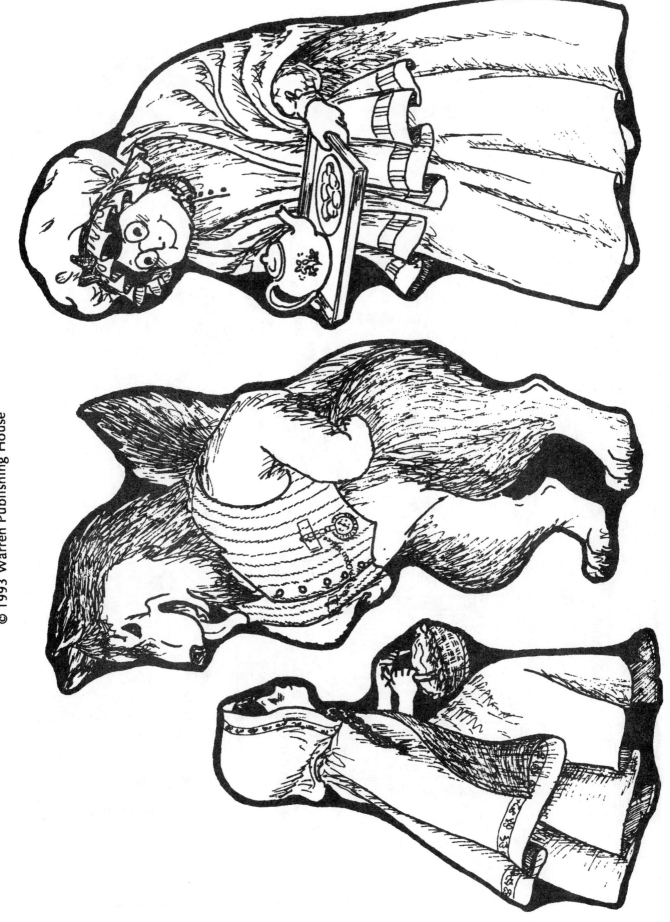

102 Little Red Riding Hood

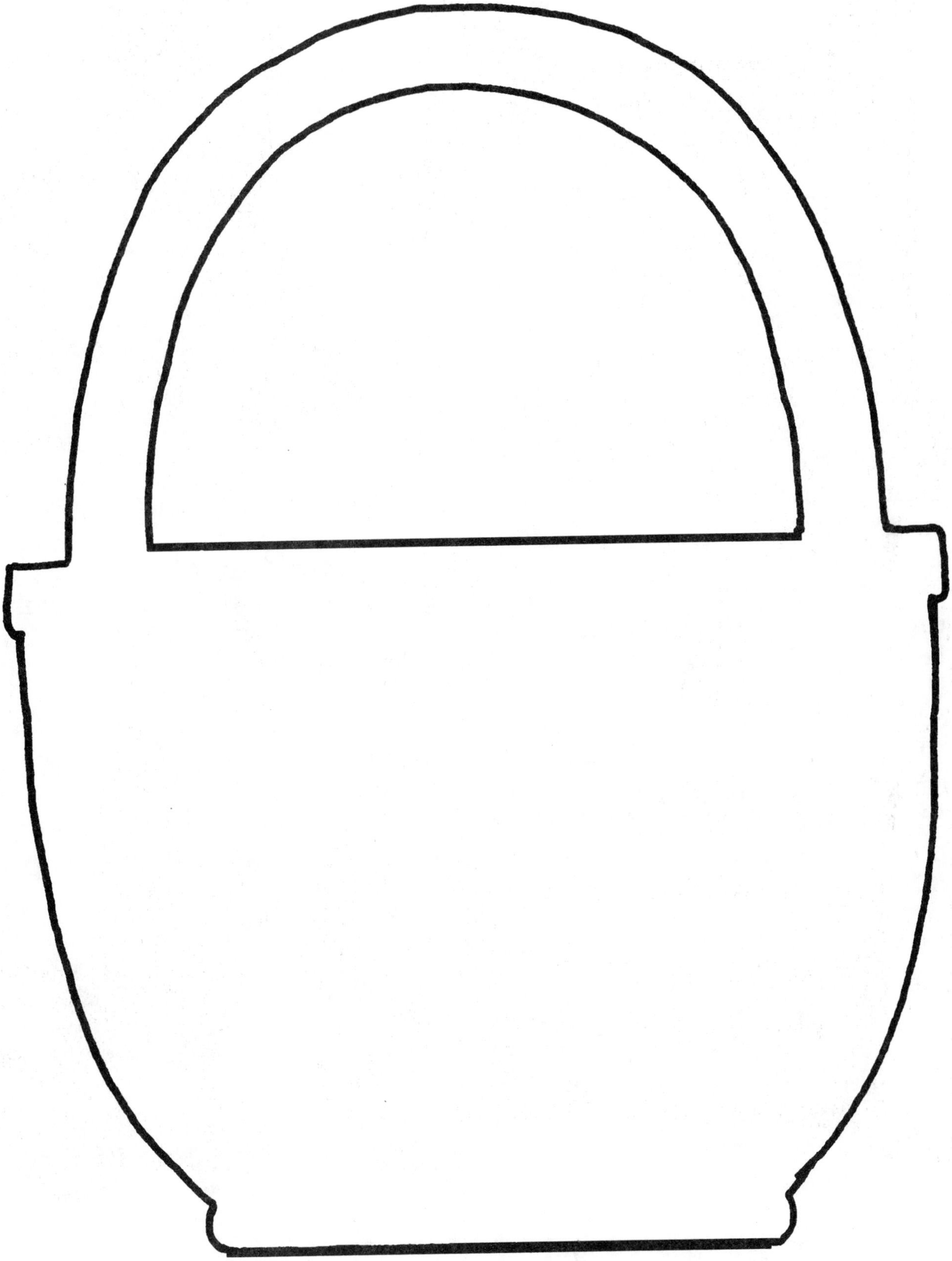

Stone Soup

Adapted by Jean Warren

Once upon a time a beggar came to a small village. He went from door to door asking for food.

Everywhere he went, people complained that they were too poor and did not have any food to share.

The beggar said that he was sorry the village was so short of food and that if the people would lend him a large pot, he would show them how to make stone soup.

All the villagers gathered around, because they wanted to learn how to make soup from a stone.

One of the villagers ran off and came back carrying a large pot. He helped the beggar fill the pot with water and place it over a hot fire.

The beggar then searched the village grounds until he found a stone that was just right.

He washed the stone until it was ever so clean. Then he dropped the stone into the pot of water.

Another villager brought him a big spoon, and the beggar began to stir the soup.

Stir, stir, sniff, sniff.

"Umm," he said. "This soup is going to be very good, but it would be even better if it had a carrot in it."

Quickly, a villager ran off and came back with a carrot.

The beggar chopped up the carrot and put it into the soup.

Stir, stir, sniff, sniff.

"Umm," he said. "This soup is going to be very good, but it would be even better if it had a potato in it."

Quickly, a villager ran off and came back with a potato.

The beggar chopped up the potato and put it into the soup.

Stir, stir, sniff, sniff.

"Umm," he said. "This soup is going to be very good, but it would be even better if it had a tomato in it."

Quickly, a villager ran off and came back with a tomato.

The beggar chopped up the tomato and put it into the soup.

Stir, stir, sniff, sniff.

"Umm," he said. "This soup is going to be very good, but it would be even better if it had an onion in it."

Quickly, a villager ran off and came back with an onion.

The beggar chopped up the onion and put it into the soup.

Stir, stir, sniff, sniff.

"Umm," he said. "This soup is going to be very good, but it would be even better if it had some broth in it."

Quickly, a villager ran off and came back with some beef broth.

The beggar added the broth to the soup.

Stir, stir, sniff, sniff.

"Umm," he said. "My stone soup is done. Now I will share it with all of you."

Everyone in the village was amazed that the beggar was so generous.

He shared his soup. He shared his recipe.

"We owe him a lot," said the villagers.

And from that day on, they never again let a beggar go hungry from their village.

Pots of Soup

Use the pattern on page 115 as a guide to cut a large soup-pot shape out of light-brown construction paper for each child. Slice vegetables, such as carrots, potatoes, turnips and celery, into thick sections to use as paint stamps. Make paint pads by placing folded paper towels in shallow containers and pouring on small amounts of tempera paint (orange for carrots, brown for potatoes, white for turnips, green for celery, etc.). Then let your children dip the cut surfaces of the vegetables into the paint and press them on their soup-pot shapes to make prints.

Variation: Let your children tear pictures of vegetables out of magazines or seed catalogs and glue them on their soup-pot shapes.

Playdough Fun

Set out various colors of playdough along with an old cooking pot. Invite your children to use the playdough to make different kinds of "soup vegetables." For example, let them make peas by rolling green playdough into tiny balls. Or have them make carrot slices by rolling orange playdough into small balls and then flattening them with their hands. Encourage the children to think of other kinds of vegetable shapes to create. When they have finished, let them place their playdough vegetables in the cooking pot. Have them add a playdough "stone" to the pot, if desired.

Soup List

With your children, make a list of as many soups as they can name. Write the list on a long piece of paper and attach it to a wall at the children's eye level. Read through the list with the group. Let the children decorate the list with crayons or felt-tip markers. Or have them glue on soup labels cut from cans or packages.

Flannelboard Fun

Make copies of the patterns on pages 113-114. Color the patterns and cover them with clear self-stick paper, if desired. Then cut them out and glue felt strips on the backs. Encourage your children to use the pattern cutouts on a flannelboard to retell the story "Stone Soup."

Vegetable Man

Recite the open-ended story that follows and let your children take turns filling in the blanks.

While I was walking down the street,
A vegetable man I happened to meet.
His head was a bumpy _____.
His arms were long _____.
His body was a large _____.
His legs were two green _____.
His feet were two round _____.
His fingers and toes were red _____.
He looked so good that, on a hunch,
I invited the vegetable man home for lunch!

Jean Warren

Color Match-up

In a basket, place several different colored vegetables (a carrot, a potato, a yellow squash, a zucchini, a tomato, etc.). Set out squares of construction paper that match the colors of the vegetables. Let your children take turns removing the vegetables from the basket and placing them on the matching colored squares.

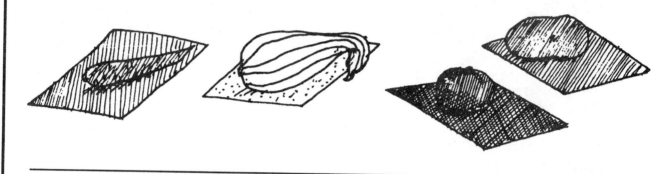

Stone Sorter

Make a Stone Sorter by cutting four or five holes, from large to small, in the lid of a sturdy shoe box. Give your children a number of stones of different sizes. Let them sort the stones in the Stone Sorter by placing each one through the hole closest to its size.

Movement Game

Let five children at a time pretend to be vegetables swimming in a big pot of soup. (Or start the game with any number of children.) As you recite the following rhyme, signal one "vegetable" at a time to jump out of the pot.

Five little vegetables
In a soup pot,
One jumped out
When it got too hot.

Four little vegetables
Swimming in the pot,
One jumped out
When it got too hot.

Three little vegetables
Swimming in the pot,
One jumped out
When it got too hot.

Two little vegetables
Swimming in the pot,
One jumped out
When it got too hot.

One little vegetable
Swimming in the pot,
It jumped out
When it got too hot.

No little vegetables
Swimming in the pot,
Watch out now,
It's REALLY hot!

Blub, blub, blub!

Jean Warren

Role-Playing Fun

Let your children act out the story "Stone Soup" while you narrate. Shorten the story (or expand it by having the beggar add more vegetables to the soup) so that there are just the right number of parts for your group. For props, set out a cooking pot, a mixing spoon, a stone, real vegetables (or paper vegetable shapes) and a container for holding pretend beef broth.

Making Stone Soup Today
Sung to: "Ten Little Indians"

Pick up a stone and put it in the pot,
Pick up a stone and put it in the pot,
Pick up a stone and put it in the pot,
Making stone soup today.

Pick up a carrot and put it in the pot,
Pick up a carrot and put it in the pot,
Pick up a carrot and put it in the pot,
Making stone soup today.

Continue with similar verses, letting
your children name other ingredients for
the soup.

Jean Warren

The Soup Is Boiling Up
Sung to: "The Farmer in the Dell"

The soup is boiling up,
The soup is boiling up.
Stir slow, around we go,
The soup is boiling up.

First we make the broth,
First we make the broth.
Stir slow, around we go,
The soup is boiling up.

Now we add some carrots,
Now we add some carrots.
Stir slow, around we go,
The soup is boiling up.

Continue with similar verses, using
other vegetable names. Have the children stand around a large imaginary
pot and pretend to stir the soup as they
sing.

Jean Warren

Stone Collection

Take your children on a walk to collect different varieties of stones. When you return, let the children sort the stones by size, color, markings, etc. Have them wash the stones and examine them with a magnifying glass. Or let them try scraping the stones with a metal nail to determine if the stones are hard or soft.

From Raw to Cooked

Have your children observe as you cook vegetables such as peas, carrots or tomatoes. What happens to the vegetables as they are cooked? Let the children sample the raw and cooked vegetables. Encourage them to compare and discuss the tastes and appearances. How are the raw and cooked vegetables alike? How are they different?

Preparing Vegetables

Invite your children to bring in different kinds of fresh vegetables such as carrots, potatoes, onions, zucchini, tomatoes and celery (or provide the vegetables yourself). Set out scrubbers or vegetable brushes and metal spoons. Have the children wash and scrub their vegetables. Show them how to use the spoons to scrape off the skins of vegetables such as carrots and new potatoes. Then chop the vegetables and let the children place them in a pot of water for making Stone Soup (see activity on this page) or any kind of vegetable soup.

Stone Soup

Pour 2 or more quarts of water into a large pot. Let your children put in a round, smooth stone that has been scrubbed and then boiled in a separate pan of water. Add chopped vegetables such as carrots, potatoes, tomatoes, onions and celery. Bring to a boil and let simmer, covered, for about 45 minutes. When the vegetables are tender, add powdered broth and seasonings to taste. If desired, stir in small pieces of cooked meat or chicken before serving.

Stone Soup   113

Stone Soup 115

The Three Bears

Adapted by Jean Warren

Once upon a time there were three bears — Papa Bear, Mama Bear and Baby Bear. They lived together in a cottage in the woods.

One day, Mama Bear made some porridge for breakfast. The porridge was too hot to eat, so the bears went for a walk in the woods.

While they were gone, a little girl named Goldilocks walked by their cottage and peeked inside. She saw the porridge on the table.

Goldilocks was very hungry, so she went into the cottage to taste the porridge.

First, she tried the porridge in Papa Bear's large bowl, but it was too hot.

Next, she tried the porridge in Mama Bear's medium-sized bowl, but it was too cold.

Finally, she tried the porridge in Baby Bear's small bowl, and it was just right. So she ate it all up.

Then Goldilocks decided to sit down and rest.

First, she tried Papa Bear's large chair, but it was too hard.

Next, she tried Mama Bear's medium-sized chair, but it was too soft.

Finally, she tried Baby Bear's small chair, and it was just right. So she sat down.

But Goldilocks was too heavy, and the little chair broke all to pieces.

Then Goldilocks decided to go into the bedroom and take a nap.

First, she tried Papa Bear's large bed, but it was too high.

Next, she tried Mama Bear's medium-sized bed, but it was too low.

Finally, she tried Baby Bear's small bed, and it was just right. So she lay down and fell asleep.

After a while, the three bears returned from their walk.

"Someone's been eating my porridge," said Papa Bear.

"Someone's been eating my porridge," said Mama Bear.

"Someone's been eating my porridge and has eaten it all up!" cried Baby Bear.

The three bears looked around the room.

"Someone's been sitting in my chair," said Papa Bear.

"Someone's been sitting in my chair," said Mama Bear.

"Someone's been sitting in my chair and has broken it to pieces!" cried Baby Bear.

Then the three bears went into the bedroom.

"Someone's been sleeping in my bed," said Papa Bear

"Someone's been sleeping in my bed," said Mama Bear.

"Someone's been sleeping in my bed and here she is!" cried Baby Bear.

Just then, Goldilocks woke up and saw the three bears. She jumped out of bed and ran out the door.

Baby Bear hoped that Goldilocks would come back and play. But she never returned to the three bears' cottage in the woods.

"The Three Bears" Finger Puppets

Help each of your children make finger puppets to represent Goldilocks, Papa Bear, Mama Bear and Baby Bear.

Goldilocks Puppets — To make each puppet, start with a 5-by-7-inch rectangle cut from construction paper. Fold the rectangle in half lengthwise, then in half again to make a long narrow strip. Curl one end of the strip halfway down to form a loop and secure it with a paper clip as shown in the illustration. Let the children use felt-tip markers to draw faces on the loops. Then have them complete their Goldilocks puppets by tying pieces of yellow yarn through the tops of the loops for hair.

Three Bears Puppets — For each set of bear puppets, cut rectangles out of brown construction paper in these sizes: 5 by 7 inches; 5 by 6 inches; and 5 by 5 inches. Fold and paper-clip each rectangle as described in the directions for making Goldilocks puppets. Have the children add bear faces with black felt-tip markers. To complete their bear puppets, let them glue on construction- paper ear shapes.

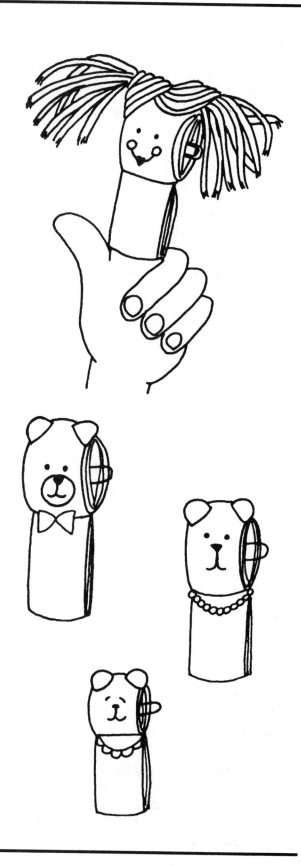

Webbing the Story

Have your children sit in a wide circle. Sit in the center of the circle, holding a ball of yarn. Start retelling the story of the three bears by saying, "Once upon a time there were three bears." While holding onto the yarn end, pass the ball of yarn to a child in the circle. Have that child say a few words or sentences to continue the story. Then while holding onto the yarn, have the child pass the yarn ball to another child and let that child add more words or sentences to the story. If a child has difficulty thinking of what happens next in the story, give an open-ended prompt. For example, say something such as this: "Then Goldilocks tried the porridge in Mama Bear's medium-sized bowl, but _____." Continue until the entire story has been told.

Flannelboard Fun

Make copies of the patterns on pages 125-129. Color the patterns and cover them with clear self-stick paper, if desired. Then cut them out and glue felt strips on the backs. Encourage your children to use the pattern cutouts on a flannelboard to retell the story "The Three Bears."

Bring in the Bears

Designate a day for your children to bring their favorite toy bears from home. (Have extra bears on hand for children who do not have their own.) Display all the bears on a special table. Ask the children to find a brown bear, a white bear, the biggest bear, the smallest bear, etc. After reading the story "The Three Bears," have the children choose toy bears to represent Papa, Mama and Baby Bear. Let them use the bears as puppets to act out the story.

Hot and Cold

Cut out magazine pictures of items that are hot (a fire, a bowl of soup, the sun, etc.) and items that are cold (a snowman, an ice-cream cone, a glass of ice water, etc.). Talk with your children about the concepts of hot and cold and let them sort the magazine pictures into two piles. Then have them glue the pictures on two large posterboard squares that have been titled "Hot" and "Cold." Display the posterboard squares on a wall or a bulletin board.

Hard and Soft

In a bag, place several items that are hard (a stone, a hammer, a block, etc.) and several items that are soft (a cotton ball, a piece of fake fur, a baby bootie, etc.). Let your children take turns reaching into the box, grasping an item, and telling whether it feels hard or soft before removing it from the bag.

Extension: Let your children sort the items into two boxes labeled "Hard" and "Soft."

High and Low

Talk with your children about the heights of the three bears' beds. Have them stand and demonstrate with their arms and hands how Papa Bear's bed was too high, how Mama Bear's bed was too low and how Baby Bear's bed was just right. Then take the children outside and encourage them to name things they see that are high and low.

Large, Medium and Small

Seat a large, a medium-sized and a small teddy bear at a table to represent Papa Bear, Mama Bear and Baby Bear. On a tray, place a large, a medium-sized and a small placemat. Let your children examine and compare the placemats. Then have them put the large placemat in front of Papa Bear, the medium-sized placemat in front of Mama Bear and the small placemat in front of Baby Bear. Continue in the same manner using large, medium-sized and small plates, bowls, cups, spoons and napkins.

Role-Playing Fun

Let your children take turns acting out the story "The Three Bears" while you narrate. For props, use three sizes of bowls and spoons, three sizes of chairs and three rugs (for "beds"). Leave out the props and encourage the children to reenact the story by themselves during playtime.

Walking in the Woods

Ask your children to pretend that they are bears walking in the woods. Have them show you how they would walk if they were tiny baby bears, medium-sized mother bears and then great big father bears. Encourage them to walk slowly, then fast, then slowly again. Then let the "bears" take turns leading the others through the woods in a game of Follow the Leader.

Goldilocks Song
Sung to: "Ten Little Indians"

One porridge, two porridge, three porridge dishes,
Goldilocks will choose the one she wishes.
One's too hot, the other's too cold.
The third is quite delicious.

One chair, two chairs, three wooden chairs,
They all belong to the three bears.
Goldie sits down and breaks one to pieces.
Then she runs upstairs.

One high, one low, one just-right bed,
Goldie climbs in and lays down her head.
She takes a nap till the bears awaken her.
Look! She has jumped up and fled!

Ann M. O'Connell

Three Brown Bears
Sung to: "Three Blind Mice"

Three brown bears, three brown bears.
See all their beds, see all their chairs.
The Mama cooked in a big brown pot,
The Papa's porridge was much too hot,
The Baby Bear always cried a lot.
Three brown bears.

Judith McNitt

Learning Body Parts

Cut a child-size bear shape, as shown in the illustration, out of brown paper. Add facial features with a felt-tip marker. Hang the bear shape on a wall or a bulletin board. Talk with your children about the different body parts of the bear (head, arms, legs, etc.). As you do so, label each part with a crayon or a felt-tip marker.

Three Bear Snacks

For a special treat, serve your children small graham cracker bears at snacktime. First, let them each count out three bears. Then let them count out more bears to eat, if desired.

Variation: Use a cookie cutter to cut bear shapes out of bread slices. Toast the shapes, then spread on peanut butter and serve.

126   The Three Bears

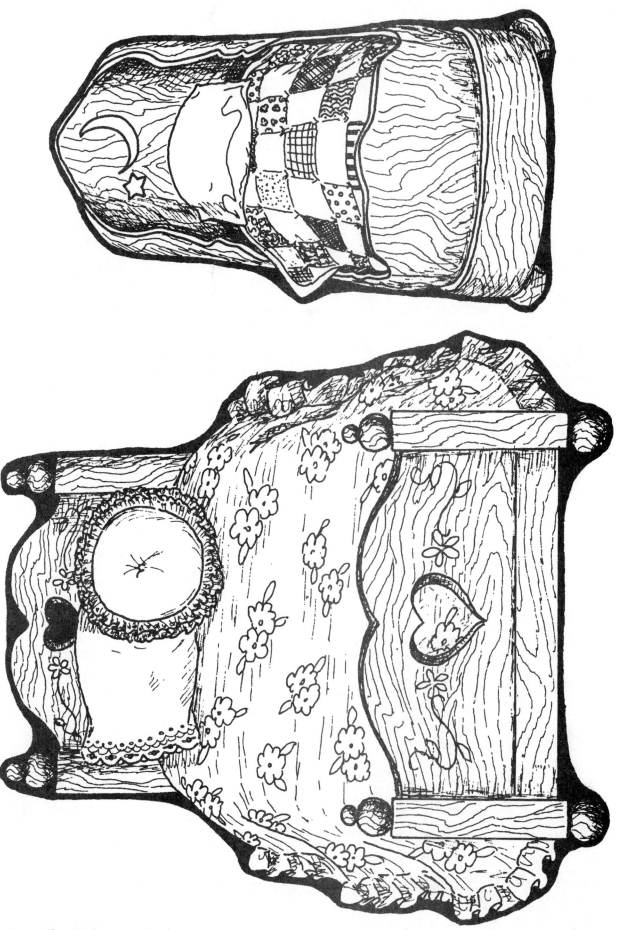

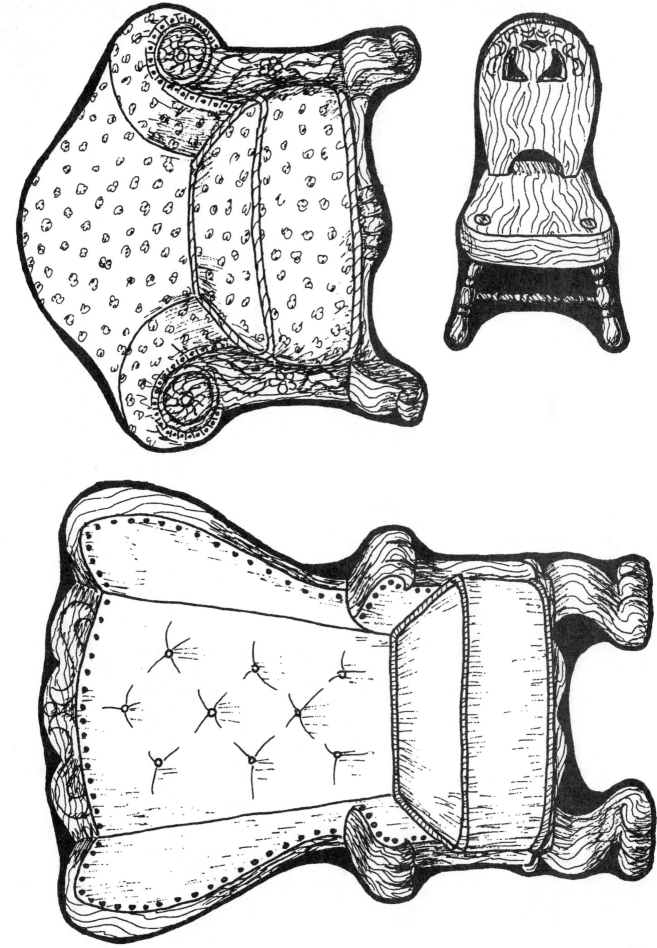

The Three Bears 129

The Three Billy Goats Gruff

Adapted by Jean Warren

Once upon a time there were three Billy Goats Gruff who were going to a grassy hillside to graze.

On the way, they had to cross a bridge under which lived a mean troll.

First, the small Billy Goat Gruff started across the bridge.

Trip, trap, trip, trap.

"Who's that trip-trapping across my bridge?" roared the troll.

"It is I, the first Billy Goat Gruff. I would like to pass over your bridge."

"I'm very hungry," growled the troll. "So I'm coming up to get you and eat you up."

"Oh, please don't eat me up," said the first Billy Goat Gruff. "I'm not very big. Wait for my brother. He will be along soon, and he's much bigger!"

"Well, all right," said the troll, licking his lips. And he let the first Billy Goat Gruff pass over the bridge.

A while later, along came the medium-sized Billy Goat Gruff.

Trip, trap, trip, trap.

"Who's that trip-trapping across my bridge?" roared the troll.

"It is I, the second Billy Goat Gruff. I would like to pass over your bridge."

"I'm very hungry," growled the troll. "So I'm coming up to get you and eat you up."

"Oh, please don't eat me up," said the second Billy Goat Gruff. "I'm not very big. Wait for my brother. He will be along soon, and he's much bigger!"

"Well, all right," said the troll, licking his lips. And he let the second Billy Goat Gruff pass over the bridge.

A while later, along came the big Billy Goat Gruff.

TRIP, TRAP, TRIP, TRAP.

"Who's that trip-trapping across my bridge?" roared the troll.

"It is I, the third Billy Goat Gruff. I would like to pass over your bridge."

"I'm very hungry," growled the troll. "So I'm coming up to get you and eat you up."

"Well, come on then," said the third Billy Goat Gruff. "I have something for you."

The troll climbed up onto the bridge and tried to grab the billy goat.

But the third Billy Goat Gruff just turned and kicked the troll off the bridge with his strong back legs.

That was the last time the troll ever tried to stop anyone from crossing over the bridge.

And from that day on, the three Billy Goats Gruff grew fat from grazing on the grassy hill.

Grazing Billy Goats

Give each child a piece of construction paper. Let your children brush glue across the bottom parts of their papers and place pieces of green Easter grass on top of the glue. When the glue has dried, set out a commercial ink pad and a rubber stamp in the shape of a goat. Let each child use the stamp to print three goats above the grass on his or her paper.

Variation: Instead of using Easter grass, let your children glue on real grass clippings.

Troll Pictures

Cut the centers out of lightweight paper plates to make large rings. Make "bridge shapes" by cutting each ring in half. Give each of your children a bridge shape and a piece of construction paper. Have the children color their bridges with crayons. Help them attach the bridge shapes to their papers with tape or staples. Then let them draw pictures of a troll underneath the bridge shapes.

Big and Little Animals

Divide a large piece of paper in half lengthwise to make two columns. Title the columns "Big Animals" and "Little Animals." Hang the paper on a wall at the children's eye level. Ask your children to name big animals, then little animals. As they do so, write the animal names on the paper in the appropriate columns.

Extension: Let each child in turn choose one of the listed animals and act out its movements. Have the other children try to guess which animal it is.

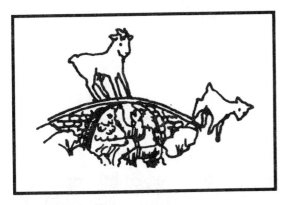

Flannelboard Fun

Make copies of the patterns on pages 139-141. Color the patterns and cover them with clear self-stick paper, if desired. Then cut them out and glue felt strips on the backs. Encourage your children to use the pattern cutouts on a flannelboard to retell the story "The Three Billy Goats Gruff."

Trolls

Let your children complete the statements below. As they do so, write down their responses on separate pieces of paper for them to illustrate.

- Trolls have _____ hair.
- Trolls have _____ noses.
- Trolls have _____ teeth.
- Trolls have _____ bodies.

Guessing Game

Have your children sit in a circle. Choose one child to sit in the middle of the circle and be the Troll. While the Troll closes his or her eyes, give one of the children in the circle two small blocks and have all of the children put their hands behind their backs. When you say, "Wake up, Troll," have the child with the blocks tap them on the floor behind his or her back while the other children pretend to tap behind their backs with their hands. Have the Troll say, "Who's that trip-trapping across my bridge? Is it you, (child's name)?" After the correct guess is made, have the child with the blocks trade places with the Troll. Then start the game again. Continue until everyone has had a turn being the Troll.

Big and Little Game

Select a big box, a little box, a big ball and a little ball. (Make sure that the big ball will fit inside the little box.) Talk with your children about the sizes of the boxes and balls. Then give the children directions such as these: "Put the big ball into the little box. Put the big ball into the big box. Put the little ball and the big ball into the big box."

Role-Playing Fun

Reread the story "The Three Billy Goats Gruff." As your children listen, let them make "trip-trapping" sounds with their hands or feet when each billy goat crosses the bridge. Also let them use their "meanest voices" to help you say the troll's lines. When you come to the end of the story, have everyone pretend to be the big Billy Goat Gruff and act out kick-ing the mean troll off the bridge.

Trip, Trap

Place a long, flat board on the floor to represent a bridge. Let your children take turns walking across the bridge. First, have them pretend to be the small Billy Goat Gruff and take quiet little steps. Next, have them pretend to be the medium-sized Billy Goat Gruff and take ordinary steps. Finally, have them pretend to be the big Billy Goat Gruff and take loud pound-ing steps.

Variation: Instead of using a board, attach strips of masking tape to the floor to represent a bridge.

Three Billy Goats
Sung to: "Mary Had a Little Lamb"

The first billy goat went trip-trip-trap
Trip-trip-trap, trip-trip-trap.
The first billy goat went trip-trip-trap,
On the mean troll's bridge.

The troll let the billy goat go across,
Go across, go across.
The troll let the billy goat go across,
To eat the green, green grass.

The second billy goat went trip-trip-trap,
Trip-trip-trap, trip-trip-trap.
The second billy goat went trip-trip-trap,
On the mean troll's bridge.

The troll let the billy goat go across,
Go across, go across.
The troll let the billy goat go across,
To eat the green, green grass.

The third billy goat went TRIP-TRIP-TRAP,
TRIP-TRIP-TRAP, TRIP-TRIP-TRAP.
The third billy goat went TRIP-TRIP-TRAP,
On the mean troll's bridge.

The troll climbed up on top of the bridge,
Top of the bridge, top of the bridge.
The troll climbed up on top of the bridge—
Then landed with a SPLASH!

Connie Clayton

Troll's Song
Sung to: "Frere Jacques"

Trip-trip-trap, trip-trip-trap,
All day long, all day long.
First I hear them tripping,
Then I hear them trapping.
Move along, move along!

Jean Warren

Building Bridges

Set up a bridge-building corner. Supply it with materials such as cardboard strips, shoe boxes, wood blocks, egg cartons, cardboard tubes, craft sticks, clay or play-dough, plastic straws, yarn and glue. Show your children pictures of different kinds of bridges. Then let them experiment with using the different materials to build small bridges for toy people or animals.

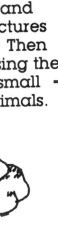

Growing Grass

Have your children spoon potting soil into several small paper cups. Let them sprinkle grass seeds on top of the soil. Show them how to press the seeds down a bit before adding small amounts of water. Then have them place the cups in a sunny spot. Have the children record the growth of the grass plants by drawing pictures each day on a wall chart.

Troll Lunches

Give your children small plates of cooked pasta noodles sprinkled with Parmesan cheese. Let them create troll faces on top of their noodles by adding black olives for eyes and noses and cheese chunks for mouths. To complete the trolls, have the children add pieces of red or green bell pepper for ears.

Grassy Snacks

Set out alfalfa sprouts along with other kinds of salad sprouts as desired. Let your children spread softened cream cheese on crackers. Then let them choose sprouts to sprinkle on top of the cheese. Encourage the children to compare and discuss the tastes of the different kinds of sprouts.

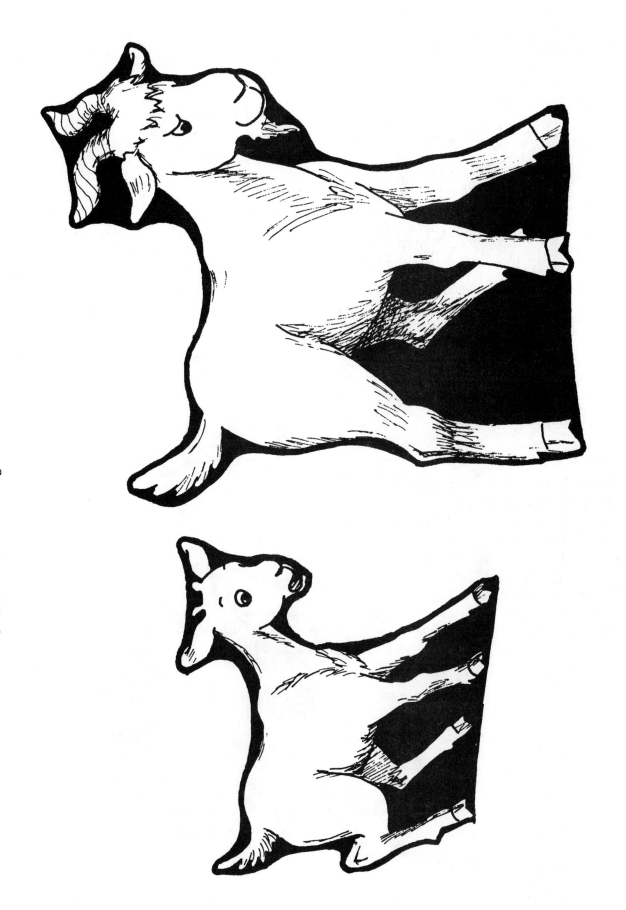

The Three Billy Goats Gruff 139

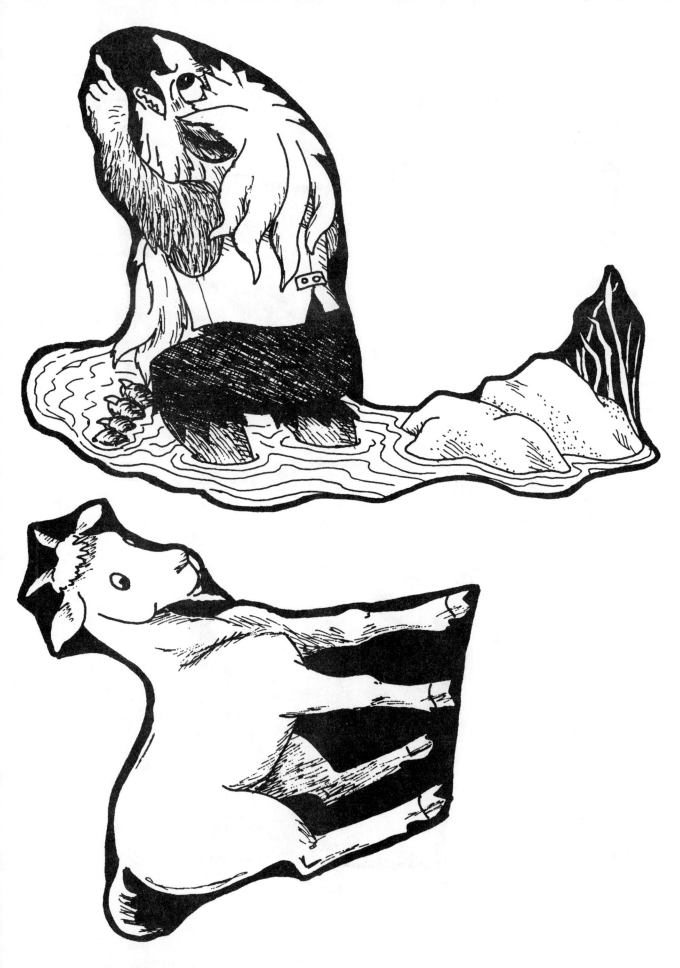

140   The Three Billy Goats Gruff

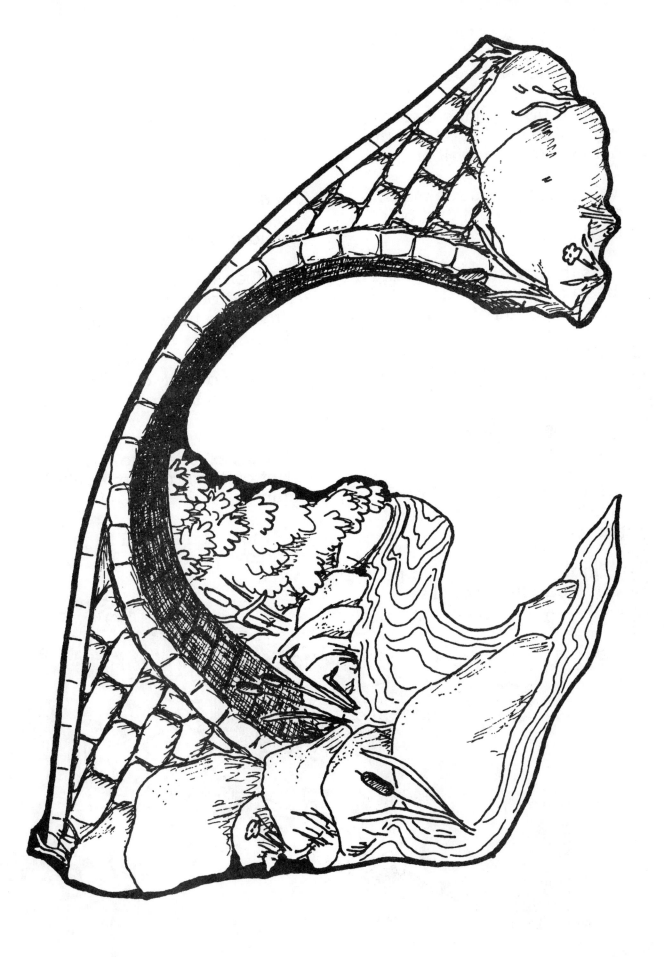

The Three Little Pigs

Adapted by Jean Warren

Once upon a time there were three little pigs who lived at home with their mother.

One day, the three pigs decided to move out and build their own homes.

As they were walking down the road, they met a peddler with a cart full of straw.

The first little pig decided to buy some straw to build herself a house.

Next, the pigs met a peddler with a cart full of sticks.

The second little pig decided to buy some sticks to build himself a house.

Finally, the pigs met a peddler with a cart full of bricks.

The third little pig decided to buy some bricks to build a house for herself.

The three pigs said goodbye to one another and went off to build their homes.

When the first little pig had finished building her house of straw, she heard a knock at the door.

It was a wolf, and he said, "Little pig, little pig, let me come in."

"No, no!" cried the little pig. "Not by the hair of my chiny chin chin."

"Then I'll huff and I'll puff and I'll blow your house in," said the wolf.

And he huffed and he puffed and he blew the house in.

The first little pig ran as fast as she could to the second pig's house, which was made of sticks.

Soon, they heard a knock at the door.

It was the wolf, and he said, "Little pigs, little pigs, let me come in."

"No, no!" they cried. "Not by the hair of our chiny chin chins."

"Then I'll huff and I'll puff and I'll blow your house in," said the wolf.

And he huffed and he puffed and he blew the house in.

The two little pigs ran as fast as they could to the third pig's house, which was made of bricks.

Soon, they heard a knock at the door.

It was the wolf, and he said, "Little pigs, little pigs, let me come in."

"No, no!" they cried. "Not by the hair of our chiny chin chins."

"Then I'll huff and I'll puff and I'll blow your house in," said the wolf.

And he huffed and he puffed and he huffed and he puffed, but he couldn't blow the house in.

Finally, he gave up and ran away.

The three little pigs
Knew the wolf would play tricks,
But he couldn't catch them
In their house made of bricks!

Paper-Plate Pigs

Let your children paint paper plates light pink to use for pig faces. Cut ear shapes and circles for noses out of a darker shade of pink construction paper. (Or cut the ear and nose shapes from pink felt, wallpaper, foil or fabric.) When the plates have dried, let the children glue on the ear and nose shapes. Have them each glue two circles punched out of black construction paper on their pig noses. Then let them glue on larger black circles for eyes.

Extension: If desired, have your children turn their Paper-Plate Pigs into puppets by attaching craft-stick handles.

House Pictures

Set out pieces of dried grass for straw; wooden toothpicks for sticks; and small, red construction-paper rectangles for bricks. Let your children glue the materials on pieces of light-blue construction paper to create straw houses, stick houses and brick houses. When the glue has dried, display the House Pictures on a wall or a bulletin board.

Rhyming Words

Ask your children to name words that rhyme with *pig (big, dig, fig,* etc.) and words that rhyme with *hog (dog, frog, jog,* etc.). Then help them make up sentences that rhyme with each of these: "One day, I met a little pig. One day, I met a great big hog."

Flannelboard Fun

Make copies of the patterns on pages 151-155. Color the patterns and cover them with clear self-stick paper, if desired. Then cut them out and glue felt strips on the backs. Encourage your children to use the pattern cutouts on a flannelboard to retell the story "The Three Little Pigs."

Pig Finger Puppets

Make three Pig Finger Puppets, like the one shown in the illustration, to use when telling "The Three Little Pigs." To make each puppet, select a cardboard egg carton. Cut out in a single piece one egg cup and two adjacent cones. Trim the cones to look like pig ears. Hold the egg cup so that the ears are on top and carefully cut an X in the bottom side of the cup for a finger opening. Paint the puppet pink and add facial features with a felt-tip marker.

Block House

Select blocks of various shapes and sizes and place them in a box. Have your children sit in a circle. Let one child begin by taking a block from the box and placing it in the middle of the circle. Then let the other children take turns choosing blocks and adding them to the first one to build a house. Continue in the same manner until all the blocks have been used.

Extension: Encourage your children to work individually or in small groups to build block houses during play time.

Counting Bricks

Have your children pretend that blocks in the block area are bricks. Let them take turns counting and stacking bricks as high as they can before their stacks fall over.

Color Houses

Cut one house shape from each of these colors of felt: brown, red, blue, green and yellow. Place the shapes on a flannelboard. As you read the poem below, let your children take turns removing the appropriate house shapes.

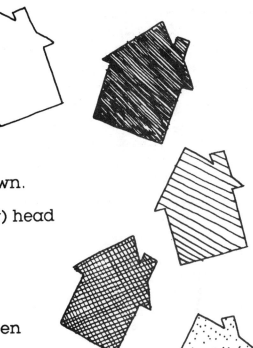

Five little pigs went to town;
The first pig bought a house colored brown.

The second pig bought a hat for (his/her) head
And a cute little house colored red.

The third pig bought a pot of glue
And a nice little house colored blue.

The fourth pig bought a crown for a queen
And a smart little house colored green.

The fifth pig bought a brand-new pillow,
And a fine little house colored yellow.

Jean Warren

Peddlers' Carts

Select three wagons (or boxes) to use for Peddlers' Carts. Fill one with dried grass for straw, one with twigs for sticks and one with blocks for bricks. Let three children at a time pretend to be peddlers and have the other children pretend to be customers. Hand out play money and let the children have fun buying and selling the materials in the carts.

Building Houses

Let half of your children be Pigs and the other half be Wolves. Have the Pigs stand in a circle and pretend to build a house of straw. When they have finished, have them join hands and dance around the pretend house while chanting: "Round and round the house we go. We tap a heel, we tap a toe." When you announce that the Wolves are coming, have the Pigs huddle together inside their "house." Let the Wolves circle around the house while chanting: "Round and round the house we go, getting ready to blow and blow!" After the Wolves "blow the house down," have the Pigs run away, form a new circle, and start building a house of sticks. Let the Pigs and the Wolves follow the same procedure as described above, then repeat it once more as the Pigs build a pretend brick house. At the end of the activity, have the Wolves run away when they are unable to blow down the house of bricks.

Role-Playing Fun

Let your children take turns acting out the story "The Three Little Pigs" while you narrate. If desired, make pig noses for the children to wear by cutting circles out of pink construction paper and drawing two small black circles on each one. Attach the paper circles to the children's noses with loops of tape rolled sticky side out. Attach long, brown ear shapes to a paper headband for the wolf to wear.

Three Little Pigs
Sung to: "Three Blind Mice"

Three little pigs, three little pigs,
Each built a house, each built a house.
The wolf came by and he huffed and puffed.
The straw and stick houses were not so tough.
Thank goodness, the brick house was strong enough
For three little pigs!

Kathy McCullough

Little Pigs
Sung to: "Ten Little Indians"

One little, two little, three little pigs,
Four little, five little, six little pigs,
Seven little, eight little, nine little pigs,
Rolling in the mud.

All are pink with pudgy noses,
They don't smell a bit like roses,
Curly tails that look like hoses,
Rolling in the mud.

Nine little, eight little, seven little pigs,
Six little, five little, four little pigs,
Three little, two little one little pig,
Rolling in the mud.

Judy Hall

Blowing Experiments

Along one edge of a table, place a variety of light and heavy items such as a cotton ball, a feather, a peanut, a book, a shoe and a stone. Let your children experiment to find out which items they can blow across the table and which items they can't. Encourage the children to try similar experiments using other items they find around the room.

Brick Wall Snacks

For each of your children, break a graham cracker into four small rectangles to represent bricks. Place each child's bricks on a plate along with a small amount of softened cream cheese for "mortar." Let the children spread the cheese on three of their graham-cracker bricks. Then have them stack their crackers, placing the plain ones on top, to make "brick walls."

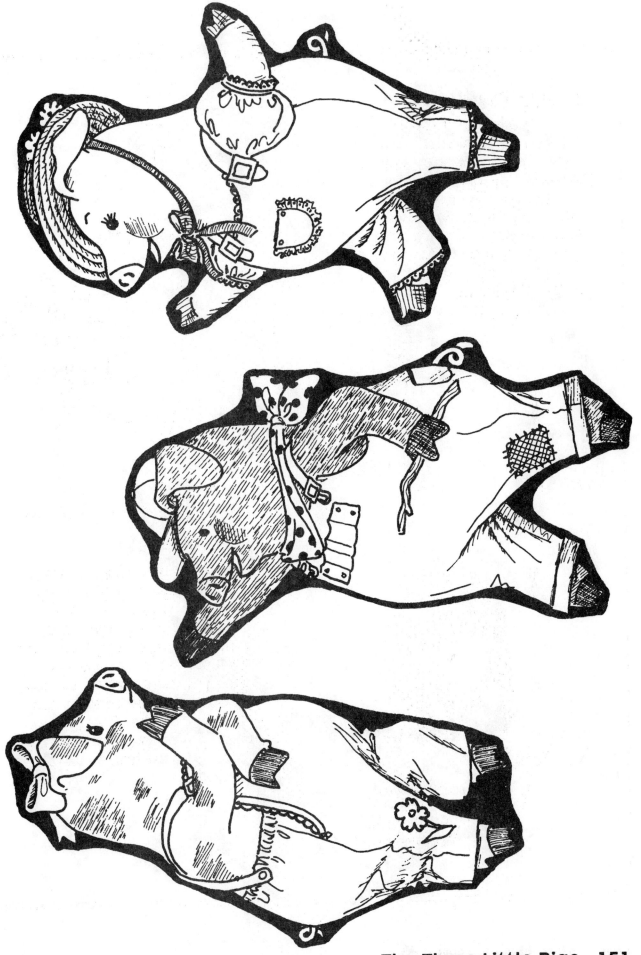

The Three Little Pigs 151

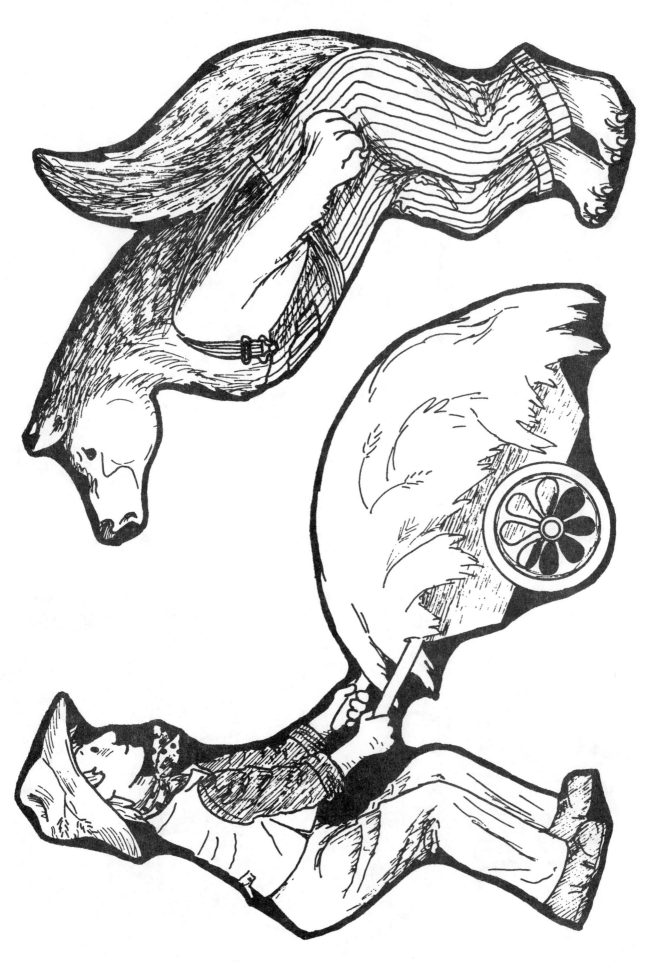

152   The Three Little Pigs

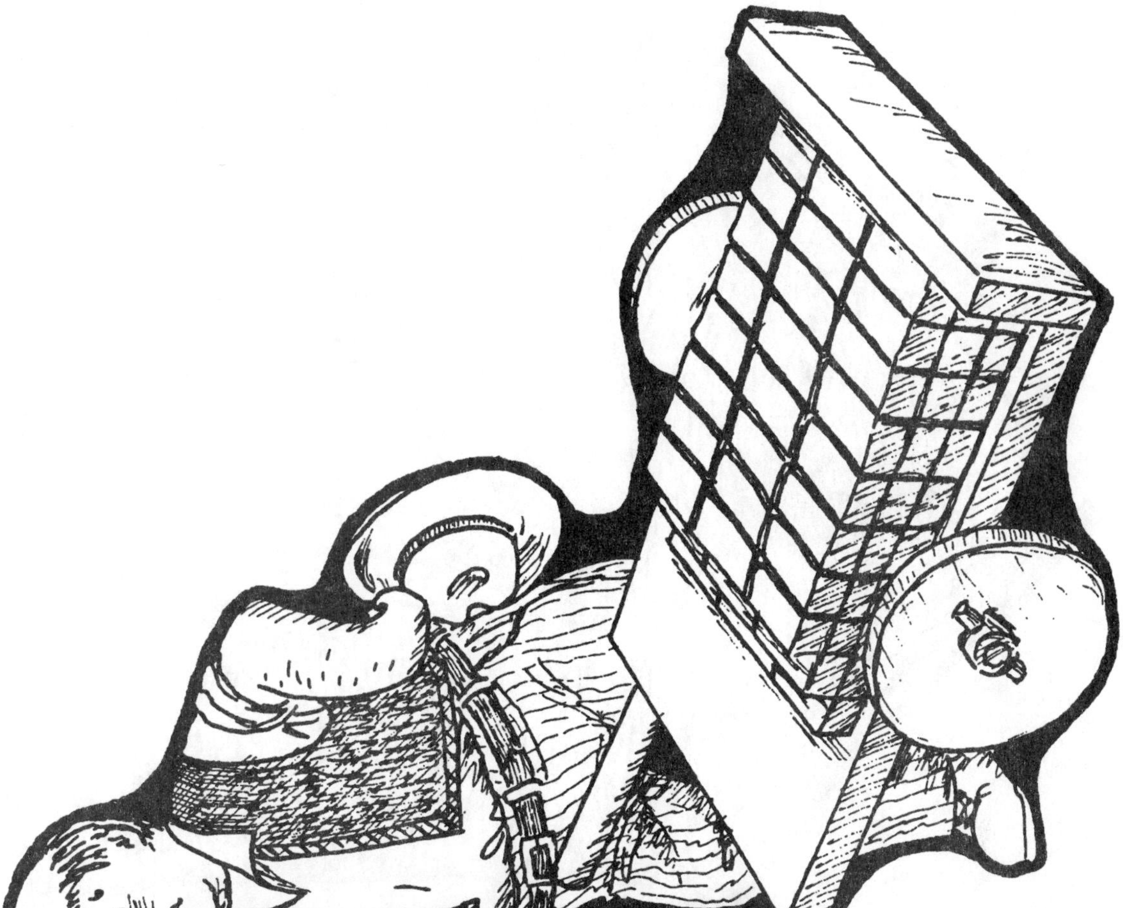

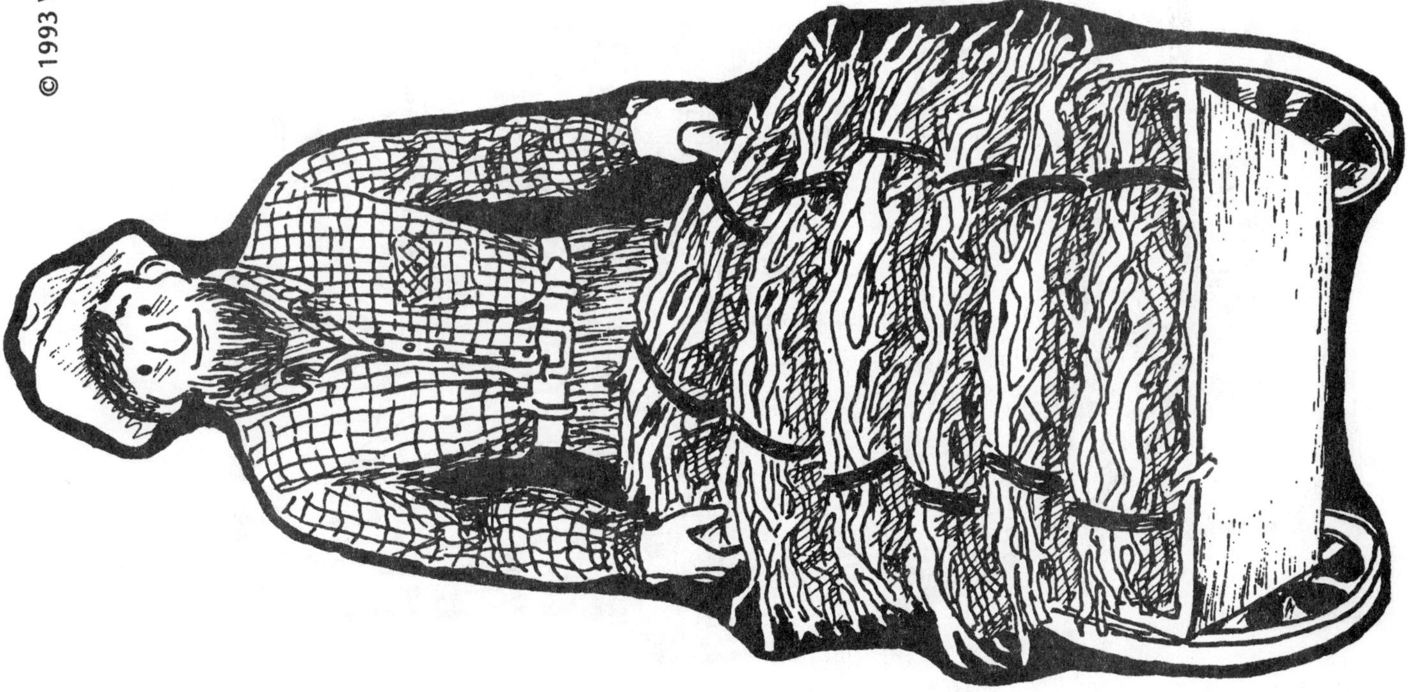

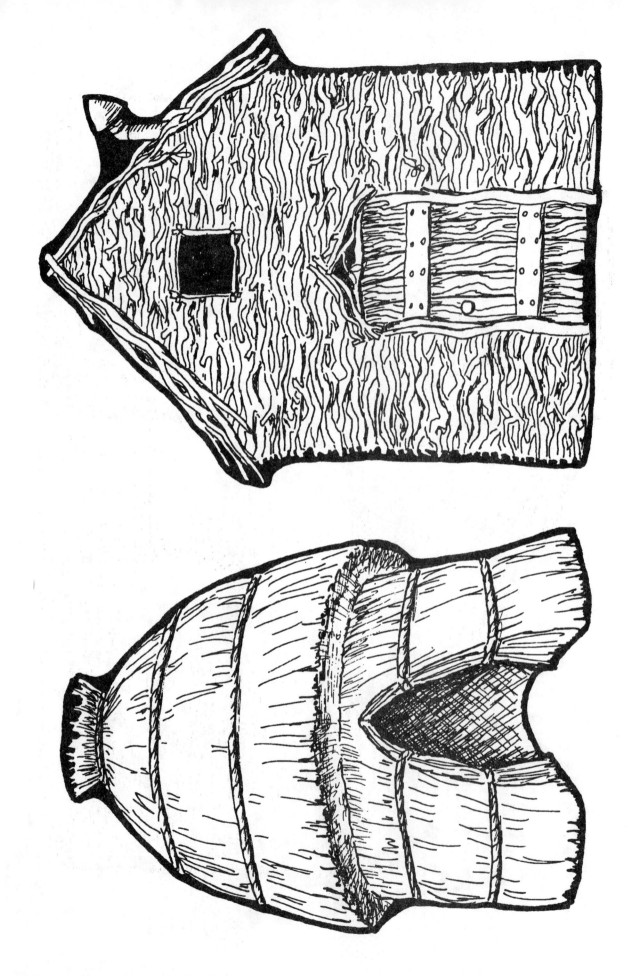

Children's Books

The Big, Big Carrot
The Carrot Seed, Ruth Krauss, illus. Crocket Johnson,
  (Harper, 1945).

The Enormous Turnip, illus. Kathy Parkinson,
  (A. Whitman, 1986).

The Turnip: An Old Russian Folktale, Pierr Morgan,
  (Putnam, 1990).

The City Mouse and the Country Mouse
The City Mouse & the Country Mouse,
  illus. by Jody Wheeler, (Putnam, 1985).

Mousekin's Golden House, Edna Miller,
  (Prentice Hall, 1987).

The Town Mouse and the Country Mouse,
  Lorinda Bryan Cauley, (Putnam, 1984).

The Elves and the Shoemaker
The Elves and the Shoemaker, Paul Galdone,
  (Clarion, 1984).

Elves and the Shoemaker, Freya Littledale,
  illus. Brinton Turkle, (Scholastic, 1985).

Shoes, Elizabeth Winthrop, illus. William Joyce,
  (Harper, 1986).

The Gingerbread Kid
Fine Round Cake, Esterl Arnica, (Four Winds, 1991).

The Gingerbread Boy, Paul Galdone, (Clarion, 1983).

The Pancake Boy: An Old Norwegian Folktale,
  Lorinda Bryan Cauley, (Putnam, 1988).

The Hare and the Tortoise
The Hare and the Tortoise, Caroline Castle,
  illus. Peter Weevers, (Dial, 1985).

The Tortoise and the Hare, Janet Stevens,
  (Holiday House, 1984).

Tricky Tortoise, Mwenye Hadithi,
  illus. Adrienne Kennaway, (Little Brown, 1988).

Henny Penny
Chicken Little, Steven Kellogg, (Morrow, 1985).

Foolish Rabbit's Big Mistake, Rafe Martin, illus. Ed Young,
  (Putnam, 1985).

Henny Penny, illus. Paul Galdone, (Clarion, 1984).

The Little Red Hen
The Cock, the Mouse and the Little Red Hen,
  Lorinda Bryan Cauley, (Putnam, 1982).

The Little Red Hen, Paul Galdone, (Clarion, 1985).

The Little Red Hen: An Old Story, Margot Zemach,
  (Puffin, 1987).

Little Red Riding Hood
Little Red Cap, Elizabeth Crawford, illus. Lisbeth Zwerger,
  (Morrow, 1983).

Little Red Riding Hood, illus. Trina Schart Hyman,
  (Holiday House, 1983).

Lon Po Po, Ed Young, (Putnam, 1989).

Stone Soup
Potato Pancakes All Around, Marilyn Hirsh,
  (Jewish Publications, 1982).

Stone Soup, Marcia Brown, (Scribner, 1947).

Stone Soup, Ann McGovern, (Scholastic, 1986).

The Three Bears
Deep In the Forest, Brinton Turkle, (Dutton, 1976).

Goldilocks, Dom deLuise, (Simon and Schuster, 1992).

Goldilocks and the Three Bears, Jan Brett, (Putnam, 1987).

The Three Billy Goats Gruff
The Three Billy Goats Gruff, Paul Galdone, (Clarion, 1979).

The Three Billy Goats Gruff, Janet Stevens, (Harcourt, 1990).

Troll Country, James Marshall, (Dial, 1980).

The Three Little Pigs
The Three Little Pigs, Paul Galdone, (Clarion, 1984).

The Three Little Pigs, James Marshall, (Dial, 1989).

The Three Little Pigs and the Fox, William Hooks,
  (Macmillan, 1989).

Story Collections
Aesop's Fables, illus. Lisbeth Zwerger,
  (Picture Book Studio, 1989).

Michael Hague's Favourite Hans Christian Andersen Fairy Tales,
  illus. Michael Hague, (Holt, 1981).

The Random House Book of Fairy Tales, Amy Ehrlich,
  illus. Diane Goode, (Random House, 1985).

Read Me a Story: A Child's Book of Favorite Tales,
  Sophie Windham, (Scholastic, 1991).

Tomie dePaola's Favorite Nursery Tales, Tomie dePaola,
  (Putnam, 1986).

NEW! Early Learning Resources

For Teachers

Art Series
Great ideas for exploring art with children ages 3 to 6! Easy, inexpensive activities encourage enjoyable art experiences in a variety of ways.

Cooperative Art • Outdoor Art • Special Day Art

The Best of Totline—Bear Hugs
This new resource is a collection of some of Totline's best ideas for fostering positive behavior.

Celebrating Childhood Posters
Inspire parents, staff, and yourself with these endearing posters with poems by Jean Warren.

The Children's Song
Patterns
Pretending
Snowflake Splendor
The Heart of a Child
Live Like the Child
The Light of Childhood
A Balloon
The Gift of Rhyme

Circle Time Series
Teachers will discover quick, easy ideas to incorporate into their lessons when they gather children together for this important time of the day.

Introducing Concepts at Circle Time
Music and Dramatics at Circle Time
Storytime Ideas for Circle Time

Empowering Kids
This unique series tackles behavioral issues in typical Totline fashion—practical ideas for empowering young children with self-esteem and basic social skills.

Problem-Solving Kids
Can-Do Kids

Theme-A-Saurus
Two new theme books join this popular Totline series!

Transportation Theme-A-Saurus
Field Trip Theme-A-Saurus

For Parents

My First Coloring Book Series
These coloring books are truly appropriate for toddlers—black backgrounds with white illustrations. That means no lines to cross and no-lose coloring fun! Bonus stickers included!

All About Colors
All About Numbers
Under the Sea
Over and Under
Party Animals
Tops and Bottoms

Happy Days
Seasonal fun with rhymes and songs, snack recipes, games, and arts and crafts.

Pumpkin Days • Turkey Days • Holly Days • Snowy Days

Little Builder Stacking Cards
Each game box includes 48 unique cards with different scenes printed on each side. Children can combine the cards that bend in the middle with the flat cards to form simple buildings or tall towers!

Castle
The Three Little Pigs

Rainy Day Fun
Turn rainy-day blahs into creative, learning fun! These creative Totline ideas turn a home into a jungle, post office, grocery store, and more!

Rhyme & Reason Sticker Workbooks
These age-appropriate workbooks combine language and thinking skills for a guaranteed fun learning experience. More than 100 stickers!

Up in Space • All About Weather • At the Zoo • On the Farm • Things That Go • Under the Sea

Theme Calendars
Weekly activity ideas in a nondated calendar for exploring the seasons with young children.

Toddler Theme Calendar
Preschool Theme Calendar
Kindergarten Theme Calendar

Totline® PUBLICATIONS

Teacher Resources

ART SERIES
Ideas for successful art experiences.
Cooperative Art
Special Day Art
Outdoor Art

BEST OF TOTLINE® SERIES
Totline's best ideas.
Best of Totline Newsletter
Best of Totline Bear Hugs
Best of Totline Parent Flyers

BUSY BEES SERIES
Seasonal ideas for twos and threes.
Fall • Winter • Spring • Summer

CELEBRATIONS SERIES
Early learning through celebrations.
Small World Celebrations
Special Day Celebrations
Great Big Holiday Celebrations
Celebrating Likes and Differences

CIRCLE TIME SERIES
Put the spotlight on circle time!
Introducing Concepts at Circle Time
Music and Dramatics at Circle Time
Storytime Ideas for Circle Time

EMPOWERING KIDS SERIES
Positive solutions to behavior issues.
Can-Do Kids
Problem-Solving Kids

EXPLORING SERIES
Versatile, hands-on learning.
Exploring Sand • Exploring Water

FOUR SEASONS
Active learning through the year.
Art • Math • Movement • Science

JUST RIGHT PATTERNS
8-page, reproducible pattern folders.
Valentine's Day • St. Patrick's Day •
Easter • Halloween • Thanksgiving •
Hanukkah • Christmas • Kwanzaa •
Spring • Summer • Autumn •
Winter • Air Transportation • Land
Transportation • Service Vehicles
• Water Transportation • Train
• Desert Life • Farm Life • Forest
Life • Ocean Life • Wetland Life
• Zoo Life • Prehistoric Life

KINDERSTATION SERIES
Learning centers for kindergarten.
Calculation Station
Communication Station
Creation Station
Investigation Station

1•2•3 SERIES
Open-ended learning.
Art • Blocks • Games • Colors •
Puppets • Reading & Writing •
Math • Science • Shapes

1001 SERIES
Super reference books.
1001 Teaching Props
1001 Teaching Tips
1001 Rhymes & Fingerplays

PIGGYBACK® SONG BOOKS
New lyrics sung to favorite tunes!
Piggyback Songs
More Piggyback Songs
Piggyback Songs for Infants
and Toddlers
Holiday Piggyback Songs
Animal Piggyback Songs
Piggyback Songs for School
Piggyback Songs to Sign
Spanish Piggyback Songs
More Piggyback Songs for School

PROJECT BOOK SERIES
Reproducible, cross-curricular project books and project ideas.
Start With Art
Start With Science

REPRODUCIBLE RHYMES
Make-and-take-home books for emergent readers.
Alphabet Rhymes • Object Rhymes

SNACKS SERIES
Nutrition combines with learning.
Super Snacks • Healthy Snacks •
Teaching Snacks • Multicultural Snacks

TERRIFIC TIPS
Handy resources with valuable ideas.
Terrific Tips for Directors
Terrific Tips for Toddler Teachers
Terrific Tips for Preschool Teachers

THEME-A-SAURUS® SERIES
Classroom-tested, instant themes.
Theme-A-Saurus
Theme-A-Saurus II
Toddler Theme-A-Saurus
Alphabet Theme-A-Saurus
Nursery Rhyme Theme-A-Saurus
Storytime Theme-A-Saurus
Multisensory Theme-A-Saurus
Transportation Theme-A-Saurus
Field Trip Theme-A-Saurus

TODDLER RESOURCES
Great for working with 18 mos–3 yrs.
Playtime Props for Toddlers
Toddler Art

Parent Resources

A YEAR OF FUN SERIES
Age-specific books for parenting.
Just for Babies • Just for Ones •
Just for Twos • Just for Threes •
Just for Fours • Just for Fives

LEARN WITH PIGGYBACK® SONGS
Captivating music with age-appropriate themes.
Songs & Games for…
Babies • Toddlers • Threes • Fours
Sing a Song of…
Letters • Animals • Colors • Holidays
• Me • Nature • Numbers

LEARN WITH STICKERS
Beginning workbook and first reader with 100-plus stickers.
Balloons • Birds • Bows • Bugs •
Butterflies • Buttons • Eggs • Flags •
Flowers • Hearts • Leaves • Mittens

MY FIRST COLORING BOOK
White illustrations on black backgrounds—perfect for toddlers!
All About Colors
All About Numbers
Under the Sea
Over and Under
Party Animals
Tops and Bottoms

PLAY AND LEARN
Activities for learning through play.
Blocks • Instruments • Kitchen
Gadgets • Paper • Puppets • Puzzles

RAINY DAY FUN
This activity book for parent-child fun keeps minds active on rainy days!

RHYME & REASON STICKER WORKBOOKS
Sticker fun to boost language development and thinking skills.
Up in Space
All About Weather
At the Zoo
On the Farm
Things That Go
Under the Sea

SEEDS FOR SUCCESS
Ideas to help children develop essential life skills for future success.
Growing Creative Kids
Growing Happy Kids
Growing Responsible Kids
Growing Thinking Kids

Start right, start bright!